People to Know Today

Lance Armstrong

Cycling, Surviving, Inspiring Hope

By Christine M. Hill

Enslow Publishers, Inc.
40 Industrial Road
Box 398
Berkeley Heights, NJ 07922
USA
http://www.enslow.com

Library of Congress Cataloging-in-Publication Data

Hill, Christine M.
Lance Armstrong : cycling, surviving, inspiring hope / Christine M. Hill.
p. cm. — (People to know today)
Includes bibliographical references and index.
ISBN-13: 978-0-7660-2694-0
ISBN-10: 0-7660-2694-9
1. Armstrong, Lance—Juvenile literature. 2. Cyclists—United States—Biography—Juvenile literature. 3. Cancer—Patients—United States—Biography—Juvenile literature.
I. Title.
GV1051.A2H55 2007
796.6'2092—dc22
[B]

2006038483

Printed in the United States of America

10 9 8 7 6 5 4 3 2 1

To Our Readers: We have done our best to make sure all Internet addresses in this book were active and appropriate when we went to press. However, the author and publisher have no control over and assume no liability for the material available on those Internet sites or on other Web sites they may link to. Any comments or suggestions can be sent by e-mail to comments@enslow.com or to the address on the back cover.

Cover Illustration: AP/ Wide World Photos.

Photos and Illustrations: AP/ Wide World Photos, pp. 4, 7, 9, 36, 41, 44, 46, 53, 56, 61, 66, 72, 77, 86, 89, 97, 101, 109, 111; Gary Newkirk/ Getty Images, p. 30; Javier Soriano/AFP/Getty Images, p. 11; Linda Armstrong Kelly/ Sports Illustrated, pp. 16, 19, 21, 23, 26;

CONTENTS

Lance Armstrong, Jan Ullrich of Germany, and Ivan Basso of Italy (left to right) ride during the fifth stage of the Tour de France on July 6, 2005.

1 MAGNIFICENT SEVEN

Lance Armstrong chopped the air with his hand. Pronouncing each word emphatically, he told a reporter, "I do not intend to lose my last Tour."[1] Many members of the cycling community and press wondered how Armstrong would motivate himself to ride in 2005. The previous year he had broken a record many thought unbreakable. He had won the Tour de France, the world's most grueling athletic contest, six consecutive times. Would he suffer a letdown now that the record to break was his own?

Armstrong's longtime sponsor, the U.S. Postal Service, had changed its marketing strategy and discontinued sponsorship of his cycling team. The team's contract had been picked up by television's Discovery Channel on one condition—that Armstrong lead the team. So Armstrong challenged himself. "I will cut right to the chase," he announced at an April 18, 2005 press conference. He would retire immediately after the Tour de France, less than four months away. "I am 100-percent committed," he stated, "and the decision is final."[2]

Armstrong was now thirty-three years old. Should he win, he would be the oldest champion in many years. Time had taken a toll on his body. He was the devoted father of three preschoolers. He found it increasingly hard to commit himself to the single-minded preparation required for the Tour. As recently as December 2004, "he wasn't focused on training," admitted his personal coach Chris Carmichael.[3]

The announcement meant there would be no backing out. He would race the 2005 Tour de France in July and he would win. To Armstrong it was that simple. Simple, but certainly not easy.

The spring races of the cycling calendar, called "the classics," revealed who Armstrong's main rivals would be. The German Jan Ullrich had been his number-one challenger for many years. But three cyclists a few years younger appeared to be peaking as his competitors. Of these, the Italian Ivan Basso was the rival with whom Armstrong was good friends. The two others were Americans and his former teammates who had left the U.S. Postal Team to lead their own squads—Levi Leipheimer and Floyd Landis.

Over the years, a number of Armstrong protégés had stepped out of his shadow in this way. Armstrong

Lance Armstrong, right, and teammate George Hincapie rest outside their hotel in Pau, France, before a training session for the 2005 Tour de France.

did not always react generously to them at first. A man who valued loyalty, he sometimes viewed former teammates as traitors. Not coincidentally, this gave him an impetus to beat them.

The 2005 Tour de France opened with a short individual time trial called the "prologue." Known as "the race of truth" by cyclists, a time trial pits each rider against the clock. At one-minute intervals, the competitors burst out of the start house to ride a measured course as fast as they can go. The day's winner is the rider who posts the fastest time.

Jan Ullrich, a former Olympic time-trialing silver

medalist, raced next to last. Armstrong, as defending Tour champion, followed one minute later. But Armstrong showed his will to dominate so forcefully that he actually passed Ullrich, beating him by more than a minute. Armstrong's time, however, was not the fastest that day. The surprise winner was an unheralded young American, David Zabriskie, another former Armstrong teammate. With his sliver of a lead over Armstrong—two seconds—Zabriskie donned the yellow jersey that indicates the overall leader of the Tour.

The first eight days, or stages, of the race crossed the mostly flat north of France from the Atlantic Ocean to the German border. Zabriskie retained the lead until Stage Four, when a crash took him out of contention. Armstrong then moved up to claim the lead.

"The man in the yellow jersey (Armstrong) is there because of luck," sniffed Zabriskie's team director.[4] Never one to miss an opportunity to motivate himself, Armstrong privately posted this insulting quote as "wallpaper" on his laptop computer. The next morning, Armstrong arrived at the starting line wearing his regular team jersey instead of the leader's yellow jersey as a gesture of sportsmanship to his young competitor. This time-honored Tour tradition shows that the leader knows that only an accident has put him in first place.

Armstrong then kept the lead for three more days. Then in Stage Eight, the Discovery Channel team

Lance Armstrong rides down the Champs-Elysees, pointing to his fans, after completing the final stage of the Tour de France on July 24, 2005.

"imploded," in the words of a gleeful rival.[5] Armstrong found himself isolated on a breakaway from his teammates. Ideally, at least one of them should have been part of the breakaway too, in order to protect the team leader from the attacks of his competitors. Surrounded by his top rivals, Armstrong was forced to fend off attack after attack on his lead. This exhausted him at a crucial stage, just as the race was about to enter the mountains. Losing time, he fell to third place in the overall classification. Armstrong, who has a reputation as a demanding team leader, was understandably angry. "What do you want to bet there'll be some very harsh words at that team dinner table tonight," speculated a journalist.[6]

Armstrong launched a counterattack in the mountainous Alps, during Stages Ten through Thirteen, and snatched the yellow jersey back once more. The race route then crossed the south of France to climb the Pyrenees Mountains bordering Spain.

In Stage Fourteen, Ullrich launched a furious attack at the base of the day's toughest climb. Armstrong stayed with him, along with Basso, Landis, and Leipheimer. In the scramble to keep up with the breakaway on a brutally hot day, Leipheimer found himself without a water bottle. He was now too far ahead of his teammates and team car to get a replacement. Armstrong quietly drew alongside Leipheimer and passed one of his own water bottles to this former

Armstrong celebrates after winning his seventh straight—and final—Tour de France on July 24, 2005.

Tour de France Records

Most Total Tour de France Wins: Seven, Lance Armstrong
Most Consecutive Tour de France Wins: Seven, Lance Armstrong
Most Total Stage Wins: 34, Eddy Merckx
Oldest Winner: 36, Firmin Lambot, 1922
Youngest Winner: 20, Henri Cornet, 1904
Greatest Winning Margin: 22 minutes, Lucien Buysse, 1926
Smallest Winning Margin: Eight seconds, Greg LeMond, 1989
Most Days in the Yellow Jersey: 96, Eddy Merckx
Most Stage Wins in a Single Year: Eight, Eddy Merckx

teammate and fellow American. Floyd Landis did too. The three former teammates then helped pace each other up the mountain. Not just good sportsmanship, this tactic was also smart strategy for Armstrong. The two Americans were far less threatening to his lead than Ullrich. Armstrong stayed in yellow at the end of the day. Leipheimer's mother Yvonne was extremely grateful. With tears in her eyes, she asked a journalist, "Did you see what they did? Wasn't that wonderful?"[7]

The next day, in the race's final mountain stage, Armstrong again had the chance to do a good deed. His most loyal teammate, at his side for all six of his previous Tour victories, was American George Hincapie. The day's team strategy was for Hincapie to race at the front of the pack. This way he would to be ready to pace Armstrong when the inevitable attack occurred.

Instead, the lead group set such a torrid pace that no attack could possibly have caught them. The team director told Hincapie to go for it. "Big George" won the first Tour de France stage of his career. "I couldn't have picked a better ending," said Armstrong. "He deserves it."[8]

"Think what 'Lance Armstrong' means nowadays. It's a universal symbol of hope. He's not just a bike rider."

Now the race was all but over. Armstrong led his closest competitor by two minutes, 46 seconds. Barring a crash, his lead would be insurmountable.

Six days later, the Discovery Channel team rolled onto Paris's fabled boulevards as the winners. The broad, cobble-stoned plaza known as the Champs-Elysees was filled with yellow-clad Armstrong admirers. Many of them waved the Lone Star flag of their hero's native state of Texas. Many cooled themselves off by waving yellow "Lance fans." One family held a homemade sign reading "Armstrong. Live strong. Forever strong."

Not only Americans had made the pilgrimage to Paris to see the final victory of the greatest American cyclist of all time. One Australian had traveled literally around the world to see him. "He's the reason we're here," the Aussie told a journalist.[9]

"More than any athlete," said retired American cyclist Davis Phinney, "Lance transcends sport."[10] Why? Because nine years before ascending the Tour champion's podium for the seventh time to say, "The Tour de France will live in my heart forever," Armstrong had been at death's door.[11]

The body of this splendid athlete had been wracked with cancer—in his testes, his abdomen, his lungs, and his brain. Doctors had given him a mere 20 percent chance of survival. Yet survive he did. Survive and triumph. "Think what 'Lance Armstrong' means nowadays," said Bob Babbitt, one of Armstrong's earliest sports mentors. "It's a universal symbol of hope. He's not just a bike rider."[12]

2

IRON KID

"You know," said Lance Armstrong, "I never really dreamed about winning the Tour de France as a kid." Reflecting on his barely-middle-class upbringing by a single mother, he explained, "You don't always have the capacity for big dreams—you don't even know what to dream."[1]

When Lance was born on September 18, 1971, in Dallas, Texas, his mother was not single—yet. Seventeen-year-old Linda Mooneyham had married her high school sweetheart, Eddie Gunderson. The pregnant bride had just completed her junior year of high school. The groom had just graduated. The young couple moved into a small apartment in the same complex where their mothers lived. Gunderson delivered newspapers for a living.

But the marriage lasted only a few months. Lance's

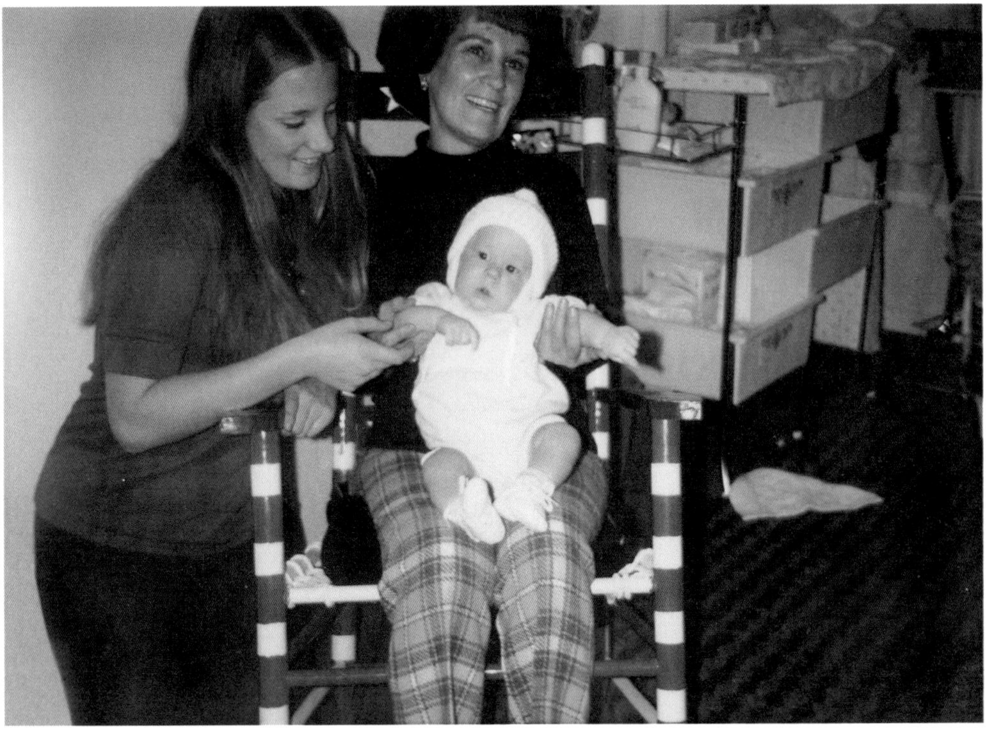

A three-month-old Lance Armstrong sits on his grandmother Elizabeth's lap while his Aunt Debbie plays with him on November 1, 1971.

mother was empowered by the birth of her son. Motherhood, she found, meant "loving someone with a love so huge, the rest of the world became insignificant . . . No task would ever be too hard for me . . . I was The Mama."[2] His father, though, wilted under the pressure. Lance's parents separated and later divorced. His contact with his birth father ended when he was only a toddler.

Lance and his mother moved in with his grandfather, Paul Mooneyham. This alcoholic Vietnam veteran quit drinking the day Lance was born.

Together, he and his daughter began to rebuild their lives. Both worked and cared for Lance with the help of family members. Lance's mother studied for and earned her high school diploma. She saved every penny from her cashier job. Eventually, she moved with her son to their own place.

As a toddler, Lance radiated energy. He walked at only nine months of age. For his second birthday, he received a plastic big-wheel tricycle called "the Green Machine." His mother remembered his reaction to the thrill of discovery. "It dawned on him that the faster he pumped those pedals, the faster he could tear around the parking lot." Little Lance wanted nothing more than to ride the Green Machine from "morning to night."[3]

When Lance was three, his mother married Terry Armstrong, a traveling salesman. Armstrong legally adopted Lance, giving him the surname that would become famous. The new family moved to a small house in the Dallas suburb of Plano. But Armstrong traveled on business five days out of seven, leaving mother and son to continue living much as they had before.

As he grew, Lance remained "a live wire" and "creative when it came to manufacturing fun and mischief," said his mother.[4] To channel his energy, she

"You know, I never really dreamed about winning the Tour de France as a kid."

signed him up for every sport and physical activity she could find.

Lance had gotten his first bike for his fifth birthday. It was a gift from his grandfather, along with its own little tool kit. A year later, his mother saw a newspaper article about BMX bicycle racing for kids as young as six. "That sounds like fun," she prompted.[5] She splurged on a new three-hundred-dollar BMX bike with all the trimmings. "It was an ugly brown, with yellow wheels," Lance remembered, "but I loved it."[6] He started competing every weekend.

His mother also signed him up for baseball and soccer. And like virtually every able-bodied Texas boy, Lance began playing football in grade school. He enjoyed these games and being on a team. But he soon discovered that hand-eye coordination and other skills needed for ball sports were not his strengths as an athlete.

Lance discovered his next athletic interest himself. His school held a long-distance foot race when he was in fifth grade. "I'm gonna be the champion," he told his mother on the night before the race.[7] She gave him a good-luck token, a 1971 silver dollar, the year of his birth. He slid it into his sock before the race and, sure enough, he won.

A few months later, Lance joined several friends on the City of Plano Swim Club. At first, his swimming skills were so poor that he was placed with the

Lance and his friend, Candice, play on his new toy bike during Lance's third birthday party in September 1974.

seven-year-olds. "It was embarrassing," he said.[8] To help improve his skills, his mother drove him to a nearby lake for solo practice. To help motivate him, she paid for a jet-ski rental afterward.

So Lance persevered. "Never quit" was one of his mother's mottoes, one she applied to her own life.[9] Lance applied it to his own. He practiced twice daily with the team, swimming a total of six miles every day. He rode his bike ten miles each way to the pool. In less than a year, he had scrapped his way to success. He became the fourth-best swimmer in Texas in his age group for the long-distance, 1500-meter freestyle event. Lance had stumbled on his strength as an athlete—endurance sports. In a long race, such as running or swimming, he could stay strong and fast longer than other kids.

At age thirteen, Lance saw an advertisement for a competition called IronKids. It was a triathlon, an event consisting of three races—swimming, running, and biking. "All the things I was good at," he said. He entered and won "by a lot, without even training." Lance already was one of the best swimmers in Texas, but not the very best. Now he was the best Texan triathlete his age. He was the winner. "I liked the feeling," he said.[10]

Though his training kept him very busy, Lance still found time to get into trouble. "I was a hellion," he admitted.[11] Tension between his mother and stepfather may have encouraged his bad behavior.[12] When Lance was fourteen, the Armstrongs divorced. Lance did not regret his stepfather's departure. Terry Armstrong had, until Lance's teen years, spanked him with a heavy, wooden paddle, even for small misdeeds.

Linda Armstrong sat her son down and seriously asked him to behave. Lance complied. "I'm rebellious," he said. "But I know the difference between right and wrong. That's because of her. She gave me discipline."[13]

Now Lance began competing regularly in junior

Seven-year-old Lance Armstrong rides his bike in April 1979.

triathlons and winning. After one event, a reporter from the ESPN television show "KidsSports" interviewed him. His mother remembered seeing him grinning and dripping on-screen in his Speedo swimsuit. "I'm just so excited to win!" he told the interviewer. "Sometimes I even get *paid* if I win, and my mom doesn't have a lot of money, so that really helps her." The interviewer then asked Lance how it would feel to go home soon and rest. "Oh, no," the boy protested, "I'm gonna race again tomorrow!"[14]

By age fifteen, Lance had outgrown teen competition. He began entering adult races. His competitors called him "Junior." Lance had no coach or practice partners. He met and befriended two Dallas-area adult triathletes by jumping into a pool with them and asking, "Can I train with you guys?"[15]

At one meet, he recorded the field's fastest swim time, defeating nearly five-hundred grown men. Though he finished at only 90th overall, this feat attracted attention in the triathlon community. The next year, *Triathlete* magazine selected the sixteen-year-old as rookie of the year. Lance could become "one of the greatest athletes the sport has ever seen," the magazine predicted.[16]

Sometimes Lance still tested his mother's nerves, particularly after getting his driver's license. She remembered "continually finagling with the insurance agent and throwing myself on the mercy of the traffic court" for Lance's sake.[17] Her son's cocky attitude, a strength on the race course, became a drawback in front of a judge.

Lance won the national short-distance triathlon championships against adults in 1989, when he was still in high school. By then, he and his mother realized that he had a future as a professional athlete. But he had a decision to make. Should he continue competing in triathlons? Should he aim to swim in the Olympics? Or should he put both aside and concentrate on bicycle racing?

Lance had continued bike racing on the side,

Lance swims for Team COPS in Plano, Texas, in December 1984.

Triathlon

Triathlon is a sport in which athletes compete in three consecutive races: swimming, cycling, and running. The most-famous triathlon competition is the Hawaiian Iron Man, first run in 1977. Triathlon became an Olympic event in 2000.

Competitions typically begin with the swimming portion held in "open water," such as a lake, river, or ocean. At the end of the swim, racers run from the water to their bikes and quickly don their cycling cleats. In amateur races, each athlete competes individually in a time trial. In professional races like the Tour de France, they ride together as a *peloton*, French for "platoon," the group of riders. At the end of the cycling portion, the racers rack their bikes and switch to running shoes. The winner is the racer with the lowest total time for all three events.

competing against and beating adults. At a race in New Mexico during the fall of his senior year, his performance turned heads. The next spring, he was invited by the U.S. Cycling Federation to become a member of the junior national team. He would join their training camp in Colorado Springs and then compete in the 1989 Junior World Championships in Moscow.

But that would mean missing a large chunk of his final semester. Plano East High School refused to permit him to graduate. Ever resourceful, his mother negotiated with a private school, Bending Oaks Academy. "Someday your school will be able to say, 'Mr. Lance Armstrong was a graduating member of the class of '89!'" she assured them.[18] The school accepted all his transfer credits and gave him a diploma.

Then Lance was selected as a member of the senior U.S. national cycling team. The new team director, Chris Carmichael, telephoned him. He had heard that the young man was strong but undisciplined. He would need schooling in the tactics of bike racing to compete at the highest level. To do so, Lance would have to leave home. Cycling's premier events were held predominantly in Europe. It was decision time. "I looked at what I did best, what I liked best," he remembered. "Riding the bicycle. I went with that."[19]

Lance Armstrong shakes hands with Principal John Nash after graduating from Bending Oaks Academy in Dallas, Texas, in May 1989.

3

NOT THE NEXT GREG LEMOND

"That kid is strong," said American cyclist Jonathan Vaughters, "but boy, is he dumb."

Unfortunately, the kid overheard Vaughters's remark. "Next thing I know," Vaughters said, "I'm being chased around the parking lot by a guy who wants to tear my heart out. And that's how I met Lance Armstrong."[1]

Why did Vaughters consider his young colleague dumb? Aside, of course, from picking fistfights with grown men? Because the bull-headed teen resisted learning the pacing techniques he needed to succeed in high-level races. A few years before, Armstrong had explained his racing strategy to a younger competitor. "I"m going to go from the gun and I'm going to win," he said.[2] Now, Armstrong still naively believed that by barreling to the front of the pack and staying there, as he had always done, he would come in first. Wrong.

At the 1989 race when Vaughters made the acquaintance of Armstrong, Armstrong did not win. He came in third. Both Vaughters and another American, Bobby Julich, hung back, cycling just behind the brash teen who led the race. They "sat on his wheel," as cyclists call it. This way, they allowed Armstrong to do the hard, tiring work of cutting through the air. By sheltering behind him, they used only 50 to 70 percent as much energy as he did while moving just as fast.

This technique, called drafting (when following) or pulling (when leading), is perfectly legal in cycling. In fact, it is indispensable in team cycling. Members of a cycling team take turns riding in the lead, cutting through the air, with the rest of the team behind them. This method distributes the tiring work evenly.

Just before the finish line that day in 1989, both Vaughters and Julich leapt out from behind Armstrong's shelter. They whizzed past him, still full of energy. Armstrong, though, was drained. He failed to meet their challenge. He had been strong but dumb.

You might think that, in his next races, Armstrong would have learned from this mistake. But no, he did not. In fact, "I did everything my coach told me *not* to do," he admitted, "Classic early Armstrong."[3] Years later, U.S. National Team coach Chris Carmichael recalled their first telephone call. "He was completely rude," said Carmichael. "He was, like, 'So you are the new coach—what are you going to teach me?'"[4]

At the 1990 amateur world championships in Japan, Carmichael advised Armstrong to hang back and wait for a signal to attack. He briefly followed these instructions. But after only two laps, he could not stand it any longer. He had to take the lead. Armstrong grinned and waved as he passed his at first puzzled, then angry coach.

Unsurprisingly, Armstrong faded and finished eleventh. Carmichael sat the teen down for a talk afterward. Still half-angry, he was also half-pleased. Eleventh was the best American finish ever at that race. The coach told Armstrong that he admired the young man's fearlessness. If he had conserved his energy the way Carmichael had advised, however, he probably would have finished in the top three. At the premier European races, Carmichael explained, all elite cyclists are strong. Tactics make the winner, not just strength.

Even this early in Armstrong's career, Carmichael could envision him at the pinnacle of the sport. "I've seen other athletes as gifted as Lance," he said, "but I wanted success from them almost more than they did." Armstrong stood out. He was "the guy who rode so hard nobody else wanted to train with him." He was the guy with the "all-consuming work ethic."[5]

Like Vaughters and Julich, Armstrong's fellow

Lance Armstrong pedals around a corner during stage ten of the 1992 Tour Dupont.

racers took notice of the newcomer. "Lance was . . . aggressive and never afraid to be boss," remembered Dede Demet Barry, a female professional cyclist who met him in 1989. Competitors called him "King," she said. "Both those who revered his talent and drive, as well as those who loathed his brash behavior."[6]

During 1991, Armstrong rode and trained in the United States with the national team to prepare for the 1992 Barcelona Olympics. As a potential Olympian, he wanted to retain his amateur status. When in Europe, he competed as an amateur member of the commercially-sponsored, professional Subaru-Montgomery team. At an Italian race called the Settimana Bergamasca, both of Armstrong's teams were entered to compete against each other. Armstrong was torn. Though he was scheduled to ride under U.S. National Team colors at this race, he felt loyalty to both teams.

This ten-day event was a stage race like the Tour de France. Each day constituted a separate race. The day's winner was the rider who had the lowest daily time. At the same time, riders also competed to win the entire ten-stage race. The overall, or general classification, winner was the rider with the lowest cumulative time.

In a stage race, all members of a cycling team ride "in support" of a designated team leader. Instead of each member riding to win for himself, the support riders (or *domestiques*) protect and draft for the team leader. They voluntarily hold back in their own performances to achieve a team victory.

Armstrong's Subaru-Montgomery coach confronted him. He asked the young man to hold back and allow a rider from his professional team, Subaru-Montgomery, to win. Armstrong was riding as team leader for the U.S. National Team. At that point in the race, Armstrong was also one of the overall leaders, with a chance to win for himself and the national team.

Armstrong agonized over this conflict. He telephoned his biggest fan and most important advisor back in the United States—his mother. With both his teams racing, he told her, his will to win and his desire to be a good team member were in conflict. What should he do?

"Don't let anybody intimidate you," she answered. "You put your head down, and you *race*."[7] Armstrong did not need to be told twice. He blasted past his opponents to win overall by more than a minute. When Armstrong descended from the champions' podium, Carmichael stepped forward. "You're gonna win the Tour de France one day," he said.[8]

During the off-season, Armstrong lived in Austin, home of the University of Texas. Many cyclists lived in the area. The hilly terrain and empty highways gave them an ideal training ground. Austin was also a funky, lively town full of young people and colorful characters. Armstrong enjoyed its music clubs, nightlife, and

Tex-Mex restaurants. Always proud to be a Texan, he flaunted his attachment to his native state. During an interview with *Bicycling* magazine, he wore a Dallas Cowboys hat, a denim jacket with the Texas Lone Star flag on the back, and the outline of the state dangling from a chain around his neck.

Armstrong finished a disappointing fourteenth at the 1992 Olympics. Immediately afterward, he relinquished his amateur status. He turned professional to earn a living as a bike racer. He joined a new professional team. It was based in the U.S. and sponsored by the Motorola Company

His first race as a professional, Spain's Clasica San Sebastian, was held in a cold, hard rain. The brutal conditions caused fifty riders to drop out. Armstrong struggled to finish. As he crested the final hill, the Spanish fans laughed and jeered at him. He had finished 111th, dead last.

Armstrong searched his soul. He had a return ticket to the States in his pocket. Was professional cycling too difficult? Should he give up? Armstrong thought about his mother's motto, "never quit." "She didn't raise a quitter," he decided. He stayed in Europe, winning two races in the next three weeks. "Finishing last in San Sebastian may have been the best thing that ever happened to me," he said. "In two weeks, I'd forgotten all about the Olympics."[9]

In the summer of 1993, the Thrift Drug Company

announced an exciting competition. It would sponsor a one-million-dollar bonus to any rider who could win the "triple crown" of American cycling: races in Pittsburgh, Philadelphia, and West Virginia. Like many cycling events, it would also confer the honor of wearing a special jersey to the champion. A stars-and-stripes jersey would be the prize.

Armstrong confided in his mother that he expected to win. When he took the first two events, excitement ran high among cycling fans. Could the twenty-one-year-old win the third event and the million-dollar bonus?

Half a million spectators lined the route in Philadelphia. "Ride a smart race," Armstrong told himself. "*Think the race through.*"[10] He launched his attack on the toughest part of the course, the notorious Manayunk "Wall." The street is so steep there that city buses are routed around the "Wall" in snow. If they tried to climb it, they would slide down backward.

Armstrong still let all his emotions hang out in competition to motivate himself. "I go into a rage," he said describing how he launched an attack in a race. "I shriek for about five seconds, I shake like mad, my eyes kind of bulge." He was proud of these dramatics. "That's heart. That's soul. That's guts," he said.[11] He won and claimed the bonus.

Armstrong remembered the rest of the summer as "dreamlike."[12] He competed in his first Tour de

France, the three-week crown jewel of the cycling calendar. Like all stage races, every day has its own winner at the Tour. To the amazement of both the European fans and himself, Armstrong won an early stage. He was the youngest man ever to do so. But his performance in subsequent stages was not as impressive. By the twelfth stage, he withdrew, exhausted and defeated. The cold, daunting peaks of the Alps were like nothing he had ever climbed before.

Undeterred though, the next month Armstrong entered the World Pro Championships. This one-day race in Oslo, Norway, consisted of multiple laps over a hilly course. Armstrong had long looked forward to this race. "I always said that someday I would be world champion," he told an interviewer.[13] A rainbow jersey was given to the champ, who wore it in every race he entered for the next year.

Did Armstrong have a premonition that he

A Cycling Team

Professional cycling teams carry the names and logos of one or more companies or organizations which sponsor them, or contribute substantial sums of money to run and promote the team. The sponsors, however, are not usually the team's owners. For example, Lance Armstrong's final team was sponsored by television's The Discovery Channel. The owners were a group of businessman, one of them Armstrong himself. Cycling teams consist of twenty to twenty-five riders. The *directeur sportif* acts as manager and chief tactician. He decides which races the team will enter and assigns riders to specific races.

In addition to the directeur and riders, teams may employ bike mechanics, drivers, medical staff, and general assistants called *soigneurs*. In addition, office and financial personnel work behind the scenes.

American cyclist Greg Lemond, center, races down the Champs-Elysees in Paris, France, during the 23rd and last stage of the Tour de France on July 27, 1986. Lemond went on to become the first American to ever win the race that year.

would win? Impulsively, he asked his mother to accompany him. She had by now worked her way up from secretary to executive for a telecommunications company. She hastily arranged to use all her vacation time and frequent flyer miles to join him. In the days before the race, she took care of him the way she had done when he was a young triathlete. She did his laundry and cooked his food. She just played Mom.

Cold rain hammered down on race day, even

though it was August. Rider after rider skidded and crashed on the slippery track. Dangerous pileups injured and eliminated others. Armstrong crashed twice himself, but both times he rose and remounted his bike.

Again Armstrong rode a smart race. He followed his coach's advice and did not attack until the next-to-last lap. Armstrong charged his way up one hill, then sped down. He stood in the saddle to power over the last hill, then hurtled down. He peeked over his shoulder to see how many riders had kept up with him. None had.

In a panic, Armstrong assumed he had miscounted the laps. Had he made his old mistake, attacking too early? Would his competitors suddenly appear and charge ahead of him? No, his steering-wheel-mounted bike computer showed that it really was the last lap. He really was going to win. He really would be the youngest world pro champion ever.

In the stands, his mother had not budged from her seat for seven hours, not even to eat or go to the bathroom. On a big screen, she had seen his terrifying falls. Armstrong went straight for her when he crossed the finish line. They embraced and both wept. "We did it," said Armstrong.[14] Looking back, he said later, the victory felt like the "end of the long, hard climb of childhood" for him.[15] The hellion had become a man.

In the United States, cycling is a minor sport. But

"I'm not the next Greg LeMond. I'm the first Lance Armstrong."

the press began to notice Armstrong, now that he was world champion. Inevitably, journalists compared him to the last great American cycling champion. Greg LeMond had won the Tour de France three times, the first American to do so. Would Armstrong become American cycling's great new hope, the next Greg LeMond? Armstrong always firmly replied, "I'm not the next Greg LeMond. I'm the first Lance Armstrong."[16]

4

THE FIRST LANCE ARMSTRONG

That day "changed my life," said Armstrong of the World Pro Championships. "The expectation levels grew."[1]

At a velodrome (or indoor cycling track) in Colorado, Italian bike racing fans mobbed him. The Italians, from a cycling-mad country, knew exactly who Armstrong was. They thrust hats, shirts, and backpacks toward him for an autograph. They vied just to touch his jersey, the rainbow jersey of the world pro champion.

Armstrong had come to the U.S. Olympic Training Center in Colorado in the fall of 1993 for performance testing. Scientists measured every facet of his physiology—oxygen uptake, heart rate, blood chemistry, lactic acid production. They also measured every facet of his performance—the gears he chose, the speed and smoothness of his pedaling (or cadence), the aerodynamics of his position on the bike.

Chris Carmichael tinkered with Armstrong's pedaling style. He placed him flatter and lower in the saddle. Though Armstrong was no longer a member of Carmichael's national team, Carmichael had become Armstrong's personal coach. Their goal was to improve the world champ's time trialing. Until then, this had been an Armstrong weakness.

"I know I gotta learn how to do it," he told a journalist. But he had a plan. Recently, Armstrong had been beaten in a time trial by five-time Tour de France winner Miguel Indurain. Both men had ridden all out. Indurain had beaten Armstrong by six minutes. "If I can get a minute a year, a minute a year isn't that much. I'm 21, he's 29 . . . Then you are dealing with something manageable."[2]

The time trial is an event on one or more stages of a multi-day stage race. It features riders racing only the clock, not each other. The rider with the fastest time on a measured course wins. Carmichael's changes resulted in dramatic improvement in Armstrong's practice times. "Let me go back to Europe," he joked, wishing he could ride last year's races over again and win.[3]

Armstrong declared himself "fascinated" by the performance testing process.[4] He had only one complaint. Having had his fingers pricked for blood tests so many times made it hard for him to play the guitar.

Participants in the 1948 Tour de France parade up the Champs-Elysees in Paris, en route to Porte de St. Cloud for the start of the race on July 8, 1948. The Tour de France, first held in 1903, is the world's most famous cycling race.

Scientists found that he could sustain his maximum effort for longer than 95 percent of the elite athletes they tested. He produced only a fraction of the fatigue-inducing lactic acid that most humans do. They calculated that the energy he generated during a race could produce enough electricity to light an entire house. In fact, Armstrong's personal genetic makeup seemed designed with cycling in mind.

Armstrong nearly had the perfect cyclist's body, except for his thick neck and bulging upper body. Unlike most strong but stick-thin cyclists, he retained about fifteen pounds of extra muscle from his days as a swimmer and triathlete. Lugging this extra weight up the 15,000-foot peaks of the Alps at the Tour de France the previous year had made the race difficult for him.

But even with his outstanding physical attributes, Armstrong's greatest strength was mental, not physical. "Mentally," said Coach Carmichael, "he just doesn't give up."[5]

As world champion, Armstrong entered the 1994 season full of confidence. "I expected to win everything," he said. "I didn't." The rainbow jersey came with a target on the back. Now his competitors were gunning for him. No longer was he a rookie whose presence in a race posed no threat to the top riders. Now they prepared for races with the goal of beating him. And they did. "I wasn't prepared for that," he admitted.[6]

Two near-misses lifted his spirits somewhat. At the Clasica San Sebastian, where he had placed a humiliating last just two years before, he came in second. In his second-place performance at the Tour DuPont, Armstrong took fourth in the time trial, a personal best.

Carmichael analyzed this improvement. "He's always used other people as a big stimulus," he said of Armstrong, "But in a TT [time trial] they aren't there. . . . It's a different psychology. Lance has to learn to race against himself."[7]

Once again, Armstrong only completed a few stages of the Tour de France. "I don't have the miles inside me yet" to complete the race, he said. His Motorola team coach and surrogate father, Jim Ochowicz, added, "You don't just go and win" the Tour de France. "It's a process of testing limits, learning. That is what Lance has to

History of Bicycle Racing

In 1868, Englishman Dr. James Moore won the world's first bicycle race, held in Paris, France. He rode a rubber-tired bike sporting the the newly-invented ball bearing. One of the sport's first international super-stars was African-American Major Taylor who reached the peak of the sport.

In 1902, Parisian publisher Henri Desgrange announced that his newspaper *L'Auto* would sponsor a bicycle race that would circle the country. The Tour de France, held the next summer, created a sensation. Only twenty-one of the sixty riders who began the race were able to finish it but more than 100,000 people met them at the finish line. Except for the years of World Wars I and II, the race has been held every year since.

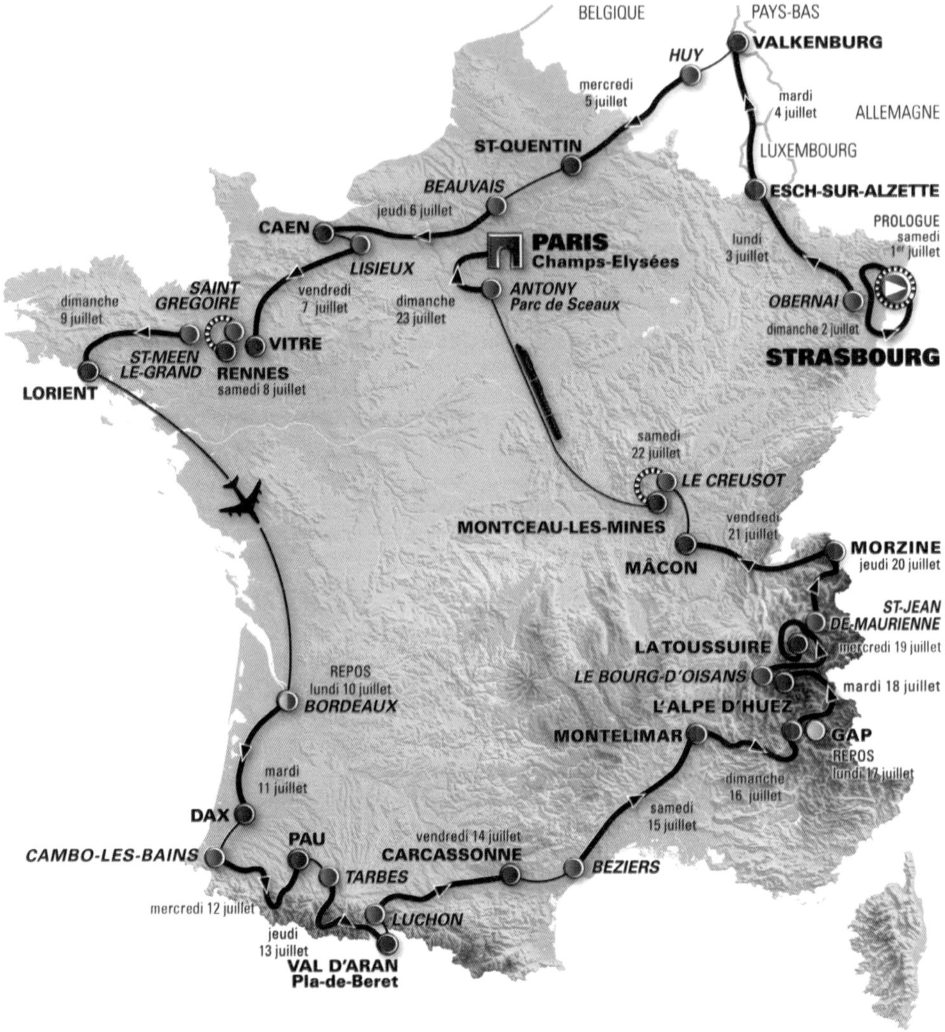

The tour de France race is held in "stages" that take place over the course of about three weeks. The route of the race changes from year to year. The map above displays the route of the 2006 race.

do." Carmichael predicted, "His ability is like an iceberg. Two thirds of it is under the surface. It will take two more years to come out."[8]

In 1995, Armstrong inched closer to the top of his sport. He won the Clasica San Sebastian and the Tour DuPont. He had placed second in both these races the year before. But tragedy struck Team Motorola at the Tour de France. Team member Fabio Casartelli crashed in a high-speed descent and died of head injuries. It was Armstrong's first brush with the death of someone close to him. "I simply didn't think I had the heart to ride a bike," he said.[9]

Casartelli's young widow, mother of a month-old baby, visited the team that night. She urged them to keep riding, saying she believed her husband would have wished it. The following day, by consensus, all the competitors rode the course. But instead of racing, they formed a procession led by the Motorola team members and their team car. Atop the car was mounted Casartelli's empty bike, hung with a black ribbon.

When racing resumed, Armstrong knew that he would finish the grueling race for the first time in honor of his friend. He knew he would win the stage ending in the French city of Limoges. This was the stage Casartelli had most wanted the team to take.

Armstrong attacked early. But it was not the foolish move of the inexperienced. It was a stealthy, surprise attack. It succeeded. Because of the day's heat, his competitors had expected no breakaways until near the finish line. Armstrong left them in the dust.

He had always loved the moment of crossing the finish line. "That feeling," he said. "If I could bottle that up and sell it I'd be the richest man in the world."[10] Like many American athletes, he showed his emotion celebrating victory. In past races, he had pumped his fist and blown kisses to the crowd. Europeans typically disapproved of this type of display. Today his celebration was more dignified. He raised his eyes to the sky and pointed one finger heavenward.

Would 1996 be the year Armstrong's talent would

Lance Armstrong stretches out as he rides alongside Greg Lemond during the fifth stage of the 81st Tour de France on July 7, 1994.

fully emerge, as Carmichael had predicted? He won the Clasica San Sebastian and the Tour DuPont for the second consecutive times. In May, he was named the number-one pro cyclist in the world.

At the Tour DuPont, a new phenomenon appeared—Lance fans. At one sunny day's stage, five bikini-clad teenage girls each adorned her tummy with a letter to spell out L-A-N-C-E. On a chilly, rainy day stage, two shirtless older men spelled out "Lance" and "Armstrong" on their somewhat larger bellies. As at many stage races, the overall leader at the Tour DuPont wore a yellow jersey. This prize also allows fans to spot him more easily as the peloton whizzes by. In one small town, a local group of military reenactors attended the race armed with vintage muskets. "We have standing orders not to shoot the one in the yellow jersey [Armstrong]. The others are fair game," joked one.[11]

The sensation of winning: "If I could bottle that up and sell it, I'd be the richest man in the world."

Now the peloton regarded him differently. No longer did his competitors merely prepare for him. His competitors had begun to fear him. Said the world's number-two cyclist, the Swiss Tony Rominger, "He is Superman."[12]

But the remainder of the year did not go as Armstrong planned. He started strong at the Tour de

France but became ill with bronchitis and pulled out. In 1996, professional cyclists were permitted to compete in the Olympic games for the first time. But Armstrong took a disappointing sixth in the time trial and twelfth in the road race.

Despite this, Armstrong remained optimistic. In September, he celebrated his twenty-fifth birthday. He threw himself a party at his new house. He had moved out of his bachelor pad with the red-white-and-blue longhorn skull over the mantle. Now he owned a spacious custom-designed home on the shores of Lake Austin. He and his friends planned to move en masse from the party to a Jimmy Buffett concert. When his mother arrived at the party, Armstrong placed a frosty drink in her hand. He hugged her and said, "Mom, I'm the happiest man in the world."[13]

5 CANCER PICKED THE WRONG GUY

"Mom, where's my flashlight?" Armstrong had phoned to ask his mother this question because she had organized the move to his new house while he had been out of the country. She told him the location, then asked, "What's going on?"

"Oh, nothing," he answered casually.[1]

But Armstrong's frame of mind was far from casual at that moment. He had just coughed up a sinkful of blood. For some months, he had felt unwell. However, like many athletes, he possessed an extremely high tolerance for pain. Every time it occurred, he had brushed off his discomfort. He rationalized that he had just had a bad day on the bike.

Dr. Rick Parker needed the flashlight to see down

Armstrong's throat. Parker, Armstrong's personal physician and neighbor, had rushed over in response to Armstrong's panicked call. Embarrassed and fearful, Armstrong had drained the sink of blood before Parker's arrival. Now he said nothing about it. Parker was unable to see an obvious problem. He guessed that Armstrong's chronic allergies might be to blame.

A week later, Armstrong awoke to find one of his testes grossly enlarged to the size of an orange. Dr. Parker insisted he see a specialist that very afternoon. The specialist arranged for further testing at once. Armstrong underwent an X-ray and a CAT scan test. An "icy feeling," Armstrong said, took hold of him.[2]

Darkness had fallen and office hours were long over when he returned to the specialist's office. Since the doctor had waited for him, Armstrong realized, the news must be bad indeed.[3] It was. Armstrong had cancer of the testes, which had already spread to his lungs. The cancerous testicle must be removed immediately, the specialist warned. He had already booked an operating room for the very next morning.

Overnight, Armstrong's loved ones converged on Austin to be with him for the surgery. His mother, his girlfriend Lisa Stiles, his agent and friend Bill Stapleton, and his Motorola coach Jim Ochowicz gathered. Several cyclists and others with whom he was close promptly flew or drove in.

The cancerous testicle was successfully removed.

A catheter was implanted in his chest. Cancer-killing chemotherapy drugs would be injected into an opening in the catheter in the following week. But the surgery also revealed that the disease had already spread into his abdomen as well.

During the weekend after the surgery, Armstrong began an intensive study of his disease. He read the literature given to him at the hospital. He devoured a stack of books on cancer. He scoured the Internet in search of the new and experimental in cancer research and treatment.

Armstrong made himself into an informed health-care consumer, in charge of the management of his disease. "The guy knows a lot about testicular cancer," said his personal coach Chris Carmichael. "His doctors are getting a taste of what it's like to be his coach. He asks a lot of questions."[4] Studying and analyzing his disease would also transform him mentally. "Lance never thought he was smart," said Bart Knaggs, one of his oldest friends. But "when he got sick, it turned his brain on."[5]

On October 8, 1996, six days after learning that he had cancer and five days after surgery, Armstrong held a press conference. Smartly dressed in a sports jacket and tie, he sat in front of a microphone looking somber but composed. The room was filled with journalists. Representatives of Armstrong's sponsors, including Nike and other bike gear manufacturers, also attended. Armstrong leaned forward to read from a prepared text.

"On Wednesday, Oct. 2," he said, "I was diagnosed with testicular cancer. The CAT scan revealed that the condition had spread to my . . . " Here Armstrong paused for several seconds. He rubbed his nose, cleared his throat, and blinked back tears. Finally, he resumed reading. "Abdomen. For now, I must focus on my treatment. However, I want all of you to know that I intend to beat this disease and further, that I intend to return to race as a professional cyclist."[6]

Armstrong began chemotherapy the same day. He lay in a hospital room oufitted like a huge rec room. Other cancer patients reclined nearby in lounge chairs. Nurses closely monitored the toxic chemicals flowing into his catheter drip by drip. The drugs were lifesaving but potentially poisonous. The nurses handled even the bags with heavy rubber gloves. Such was the toxicity level required to kill cancer cells.

But it promptly became apparent that more was wrong with Armstrong. Blood tests suggested that the cancer had spread even further. An MRI (magnetic resonance imaging) test now revealed two brain tumors. Armstrong had studied his disease. He knew the gravity of his situation. He phoned the friend of a friend, American track star Steve Scott, who was also fighting testicular cancer, for advice. But "compared to Lance," said Scott, "what I have is like a pimple. I'm afraid he's

Lance Armstrong was originally diagnosed with testicular cancer in October 1996.

not going to live."[7] Bart Knaggs's future father-in-law, a doctor, simply told Knaggs, "Your friend is dead."[8]

"What are my chances?" Armstrong asked the doctor who had performed his surgery. "[Fifty] percent," he answered. "But really I was thinking twenty," he admitted later.[9] Armstrong had faced long odds before. He had risen from the near-poverty of a single-parent home to the apex of international sport. "Never quit" had been his mother's motto. Armstrong had adopted her determination on the race course. Now he applied it to his fight for life. "Something told me that fear should never fully rule the heart," Armstrong said. "I decided not to be afraid."[10]

"Something told me that fear should never fully rule the heart. I decided not to be afraid."

Once his disease had been announced to the world, Armstrong found that he had joined the "cancer community." This is the circle of fellowship felt by people who have or have had cancer, along with their loved ones and caregivers. Phone calls, letters, and e-mails of encouragement and advice engulfed him.

One phone call may have saved his career. Dr. Steven Wolff was himself an oncologist (cancer specialist) as well as a recreational cyclist and bike racing fan. He advised Armstrong to seek treatment at Indiana University Medical Center. Its head physician,

Dr. Larry Einhorn, had developed the standard treatment plan for testicular cancer used around the world.

Dr. Wolff also mentioned that the combination of cancer-fighting drugs Armstrong currently used could have long-term detrimental effects on his lung capacity and balance. Dr. Wolff suggested that a different combination could be equally effective at curing his cancer and preserving his athletic ability. Armstrong decided to take this advice.

On October 25, Armstrong underwent surgery in Indianapolis to remove the brain tumors. Miraculously, the single week's course of chemotherapy he had already taken in Texas seemed to have begun working. The brain tumors were already shrinking. It was the first good news Armstrong had received since his diagnosis.

After surgery, Armstrong fought conflicting emotions. Of course, he felt glad to be alive. But

Testicular Cancer

Testicular cancer is a disease in which malignant cells grow in the testes or testicles, the male sex glands. Only one percent of all male cancer patients suffer from testicular cancer, but it is the most common cancer in men under 35. The majority of victims are white. The cause remains unknown, but men with a family history of testicular cancer are at greater risk.

Symptoms of testicular cancer include a painless lump, swelling, or discomfort in a testicle or pain in the lower back or groin area. Once the symptoms are noticed, blood tests, ultrasound examination, or biopsy will determine if cancer is the cause. A biopsy is examination of cells from the afflicted area under a microscope to see if they are cancerous.

Lance Armstrong and his mother, Linda, celebrated Armstrong's one-year anniversary of being cancer free in October 1997.

he also felt "alive enough to *be* mad . . . fighting mad," he said. Anger at his illness overwhelmed him but it motivated him. What is more, he loved feeling this way. "I *like* it like this," he told Chris Carmichael. "I like the odds stacked against me, they always have been, and I don't know any other way."[11]

The next day, he began a second and new course of chemotherapy. His doctors carefully chose the combination or "cocktail" of drugs in his drip to enable him to keep racing, should he recover. Though the treatment made him violently ill, the blood marker numbers for his illness promptly began to fall. This meant that the drugs were working to kill the cancer.

A third course of chemotherapy the following month showed even more dramatic results. "You're a responder," his doctor told him. Now, Armstrong allowed himself to feel a glimmer of the sensation he felt when he crossed the finish line—the feeling of winning. "Cancer picked the wrong guy," he told a friend. "When it looked around for a body to hang out in, it made a big mistake when it chose mine. *Big* mistake."[12]

Amazingly, all this time, Armstrong had never stopped riding his bike. At home in Austin, between courses of chemotherapy, he rode every day. Not much, and very slowly, but he rode. "I didn't love the bike before I got sick," he admitted. He loved strenuous exercise. He loved the struggle of sport. He loved winning, but he had not loved riding for its own sake. Now he loved it.[13]

The organizers of the Tour de Gruene, a bike race held in Austin on November 10, invited him to attend as a spectator. Armstrong asked if he could ride rather than watch. Eddy Merckx, the Belgian cycling legend and five-time winner of the Tour de France, was planning to visit Armstrong that weekend. Merckx, Armstrong's long-time idol, agreed to ride a ceremonial two-man time trial with him for the event.

On race day, Armstrong wore a helmet on his shaved head, but surgical scars on his scalp were still visible. When the two of them took their places, the crowd roared its approval. "If I said I didn't cry on the starting line," admitted Armstrong, "I'd be lying."[14]

6

VIVA LANCE

One day, the head cancer nurse asked Armstrong to speak to a young boy about to undergo chemotherapy for the first time. While visiting and reassuring him, Armstrong showed the boy his driver's license. The Department of Motor Vehicles photograph on it pictured an Armstrong in the middle of chemotherapy. Chemotherapy causes patients to lose all their hair. The photo showed him totally bald, without even eyebrows or eyelashes. Armstrong wanted the picture always to remind him of the battle he had waged with cancer, even after he got well.

The medical staff often asked Armstrong to meet with other patients. They realized what an impact his example could have—a professional athlete who struggled and fought just like them. The bravery of the cancer-stricken children he met particularly moved Armstrong. He compared them to the five-time winner of the Tour de France, Miguel Indurain. "I saw children," he said, "their hair burned away by chemo, who fought with the hearts of Indurains."[1]

Craig Nichols, one of Armstrong's doctors, urged him to become an activist who gave hope and inspiration to other cancer victims. Nichols believed that Armstrong was the "most willful person I have ever met."[2] Perhaps he could use that formidable will in the service of his fellow patients and survivors. Armstrong had been thinking along the same lines about becoming an activist. He proposed to a group of friends that they organize a biking event to raise money for cancer research. They would call it the "Ride for the Roses." This effort would become Armstrong's first step in establishing a charity foundation.

Armstrong hoped that, eventually, such a foundation might continue to raise enough money to give grants to scientists testing new ways to treat or prevent cancer. He also envisioned the foundation working directly with patients. He wanted to spread the word that anyone could use the same tools he had used to fight his disease. He had gotten more than one medical opinion on treatment options. He had informed himself fully about his disease. He had played an active role in making decisions along with his doctors.

Armstrong's most important goal for the foundation, however, was showing that cancer victims could fight and live, as he had. Surviving cancer had made him a better person. Armstrong believed it could do the same for any survivor.

He took his final chemotherapy treatment on December 13, 1996. Testing at that point showed that his cancer had decreased dramatically, but had not totally disappeared. Armstrong would need monthly blood tests to monitor his condition. After one year,

Cancer survivor Michael Lin, who works at the Lance Armstrong Foundation in Austin, Texas, displays his "Live Strong" wristband in May 2004.

Treatment for Testicular Cancer

Removal of the diseased testicle is the first line of defense against the spread of the disease. If the disease has already spread, doctors test blood chemistry to measure "markers" in the blood and also use chest X rays and CT scans to determine its reach.

Doctors choose treatment strategy based on the type of tumor present in addition to how far the disease has spread. Sometimes the lymph nodes, which drain the testes into the abdomen, are also removed. Other times, they are treated with radiation or are left alone. The most serious cases require multidrug chemotherapy.

Once treatment renders a patient cancer-free, follow-up examinations are scheduled to make sure the cancer does not return. After a patient has been cancer-free for five years, recurrence of the disease is uncommon.

the doctors would know if chemotherapy had been fully successful. They would only pronounce him cured when he had been cancer-free for five years. It would be hard for a person as aggressive and impatient as Armstrong to wait. "I wanted to be cured, and cured now," he said.[3] Just three months later, his blood markers showed no remaining cancer.

The same month, his foundation's inaugural event took place. Armstrong's Austin friends and the international bike racing community rallied around his cause. On March 23, 1997, more than two thousand cyclists gathered for the Ride for the Roses. Jakob Dylan, an Armstrong buddy and part of the band The Wallflowers, played the national anthem on electric guitar. Olympic athletes and former Tour de France winners, as well as ordinary people, joined Armstrong in the ceremonial ride. The event raised more than two hundred thousand dollars for cancer research.

"Cancer changes you," Armstrong explained to a reporter who marveled at this hard-nosed athlete's newly-revealed compassion. Naturally, the reporter also asked if and when Armstrong would mount a serious comeback to racing. He felt "awesome in general but not awesome on the bike," said Armstrong.[4] He would defer to his doctors' advice. They had ordered him to devote time to his recovery.

While planning the Ride for the Roses, Armstrong had met a young woman named Kristin Richard. Everyone called her Kik (pronounced Keek). She worked for an advertising agency whose client was a race sponsor. Armstrong noticed her slender form, long blonde hair, and wide smile, as well as her wit and intelligence. Since they were both dating others at the time, the two simply became friends.

After the event, Armstrong kept seeking excuses to call and e-mail her. A few months later, he and long-time girlfriend Lisa Stiles broke up. When Armstrong called Kristin Richard soon after, he discovered that she too was now single. "So what are you doing tonight?" he asked. "Something with you," she replied.[5] Quickly they became inseparable.

That summer Richard took a long-planned extended vacation to Europe. Armstrong accompanied her. Though he had lived and traveled abroad as an athlete, this was his first experience of Europe at a leisurely pace. The pair savored food, wine, art, and architecture. They attended the Tour de France as tourists.

Back at home, Armstrong's coach Chris Carmichael and his agent Bill Stapleton urged him to consider a return to competition. In October 1997, he passed his one-year recovery milestone. He proposed marriage to Richard and she accepted. Maybe the time was right to come back. He was healthy and in love. Armstrong began to train.

He signed a contract with a new team sponsored by the U.S. Postal Service. Armstrong attended a gala New York reception welcoming him to the team. A genuine postal worker hand-delivered Armstrong his new bike and team jersey. He would no longer be the lead rider, however. He would ease back into the sport as a support rider, a domestique. "He's following his dream, and I applaud that," said the team director.[6]

Not long after, a reporter asked about the motivation for his comeback. "I was born to be a cancer survivor," answered Armstrong, "and a cancer survivor who comes back to racing . . . It would disappoint a lot of people in the cancer community if I didn't try to race again." At this point, Armstrong believed that the remainder of his career would be devoted to competing in one-day races (or "classics") and shorter stage races. His health history ruled out an overall victory in the Tour de France, he believed. "Riding the Tour would be lunacy," he said.[7]

Armstrong and fiancée Kristin Richard moved to France. He placed fourteenth in his first race, a decent showing for any cyclist, let alone a cancer survivor. But Armstrong had never been just "any cyclist." In his second race, from Paris to Nice, in pouring rain, with the temperature in the 30s, he quit. "My heart wasn't into it any more," he admitted. "I needed to go home and just celebrate the fact that I was living."[8] Was this Armstrong the fighter? The same one who had adopted his mother's motto, "never quit"?

He and Richard moved back to Texas, even though they had just relocated across continents. Armstrong played golf and water-skied. Some days, he would just lie on the couch and watch TV. He washed down his beloved Tex-Mex food with beer. Though he was not training, he did not announce his retirement.

After a few weeks, Richard sat him down. She asked him for a decision about his future. "You are deciding by not deciding," she told him. "And that is so un-Lance."[9] She and his coaches persuaded him to get fit for the 1998 Ride for the Roses, then to announce his final professional race.

To get him back into shape, Armstrong, Chris Carmichael, and a training partner departed for the mountains of North Carolina. Armstrong warmed to the location immediately. He had won the Tour DuPont twice on these peaks. But the spring weather broke cold and rainy, exactly the same conditions that

Lance Armstrong and his wife, Kristin, together in 1999.

had driven him to quit in France. This time, however, Armstrong felt cleansed by the conditions. He felt he was "staring the elements that had defeated me in the eye," he said.[10]

One day, Carmichael scheduled a 100-mile ride that finished with an ascent of Beech Mountain. By the time he reached the base of the peak, Armstrong had been in the saddle for six hours, soaking wet. He remembered the crowds of fans who had cheered him there in his two Tour DuPont victories. As he began to climb, he looked down at the road and saw something spooky. In faint yellow and white letters, he made out the words "Viva Lance," or "long live Lance." Fans had painted the message on the road years before to urge him on.

As he plowed up the mountain, he became a new man. The ascent caused him to come to a decision. "I saw my life as a whole," he said. "I saw the pattern and the privilege of it, and the purpose of it, too. It was simply this: I was meant for a long, hard climb."[11] He would return to competition. Though the rest of his career would honor cancer survivors, he would not return for them. He would return for himself. "When I quit" in France, he said, "I gave myself permission to come back to cycling on my own." Now, "I had that edge."[12]

Armstrong quickly regained his fitness. But cancer had affected his body in a strange and wonderful way. Chemotherapy had destroyed his muscle mass, including the bulky neck, shoulder, and chest muscles that had held him back in mountain stages. Now he had the lean, ropy muscles of a climber instead. "It was all he needed," said his former coach Jim Ochowicz. "He became very good in the mountains."[13]

Armstrong married Kristin Richard in May 1998. Too energized by his rebirth as a competitor, he cut their honeymoon short to train. This year's Ride for the Roses would include an official race, as well as a fun ride. Armstrong won it over a respectable field. Then he took fourth at the U.S. Pro Championships in Philadelphia.

> **"I knew exactly what I should do. I wanted to win the Tour de France."**

It was time to return to Europe. Armstrong entered and won the Tour of Luxembourg. He placed well in other races of the European summer season. In October 1998, two years after his cancer diagnosis, Armstrong took fourth at the Tour of Spain, one of cycling's top three events. More important, he won the most grueling mountain stage, braving frigid gale-force winds. At this race, he said, he had "felt more like a competitive athlete than I had in a long time or possibly ever."[14]

During the year-end holidays back in Austin, Armstrong received an e-mail from Johan Bruyneel, the new director of the U.S. Postal Team. "You will look great on the podium of the Tour de France next year," Bruyneel wrote. Armstrong pondered this message for a few days. Finally, "after a year of confusion and self-doubt," he said, "I now knew exactly what I should do. I wanted to win the Tour de France."[15]

7

THE YELLOW JERSEY

It was "a big risk, but he was a new man . . . and it was a chance for him to prove that," said Kristin Armstrong of her husband's quest for cycling's holy grail. "Nobody expected me to win the Tour de France," Armstrong believed. "Nobody expected me to win anything. I had nothing to lose."[1]

The Armstrongs moved to their villa in Nice, France, early in 1999. While her husband trained, Kristin Armstrong relaxed and rested in the Riviera sun. She was pregnant with the couple's first child. Because cancer had left Armstrong infertile, the couple had used in-vitro fertilization to conceive.

The Postal Service team director had a plan. Johan Bruyneel, a Belgian, had won a stage of the Tour de France himself. He arranged for the teammates to spend the early months of the year training on the exact mountain stages they would race in the Tour. This way the riders would personally learn every danger and challenge of each route before contesting it. As obvious and elementary as this sounds, it had rarely been done before. Bruyneel was the first to make it part of his team's standard training.

Of all the teammates, Armstrong pushed himself hardest. Every day he scaled a mountain route planned for the Tour. He stopped only when snow blocked the road. Then he would descend and do it again.

He used the scientific mind-set he had acquired as a cancer patient to hone a perfect racer's body for himself. He calculated the exact number of calories he would expend in the next day's training. Then he weighed his food at meals. He ate only enough so that his caloric intake exactly matched the amount he expected to expend. And no more Tex-Mex. His training table regimen limited him to high-carb, energy-producing grains, fruits, and egg whites.

Armstrong took second place in a Dutch one-day race in April. The loss gave him just the competitive fuel he needed. Michael Boogerd of Holland had beaten him by a mere centimeter in a last-minute sprint to the finish line. On the winner's podium, Armstrong gave notice to Boogerd. The Dutchman was a prerace favorite to win the Tour de France. "You're going to pay me back in July," Armstrong told his startled competitor, meaning at the Tour.[2]

This was a typically-Armstrong challenge to himself. Now he would have to back up a public boast with action. He returned to training with a vengeance. The following month, he broke the course record for climbing the Col de la Madone, the mountain that towers over Nice. "I'm ready," he declared.[3]

Indeed, he was. The Tour's prologue was an eight-kilometer time trial. Armstrong was "nervous," said his teammate Frankie Andreu. "Normally, he is not like that." That meant "Lance knew he could do it."[4] Sure enough, he smashed the course record set by the great Miguel Indurain by a full ten seconds. Indurain himself met Armstrong at the finish line with a handshake and hug.

For the first time, Armstrong would don the hallowed yellow jersey of the Tour de France overall leader. On the podium, he remembered imagining this victory many times. But never had he imagined the actual sensation of pulling it over his head and standing clad in yellow. Now, the eight support riders of the Postal Service team would have the honor, duty, and burden of defending the *maillot jaune* (yellow jersey in French). "When you have the yellow jersey on your wheel [pulling him], there's something special about it," said teammate Tyler Hamilton. "You draw strength from it. You know he's counting on you."[5]

Lance Armstrong rides past the Arc de Triomphe during the final stage of the Tour de France on July 25, 1999. Armstrong's victory made him just the second American to win the race.

Stage Two was held on the Fourth of July. But being the race leader made up for "not being back home drinking beer and watching fireworks," Armstrong told a reporter.[6]

He dropped back to second place in this stage, content for now to bide his time. Frankie Andreu joked that Armstrong most regretted losing access to the yellow jersey's private camper. It came with a television and well-stocked refrigerator. Reporters were not allowed to enter.

Stage Three would cross a narrow, stone causeway, Passage de Gois, between the mainland and an island on the Atlantic coast. The road was so close to sea level that it flooded at high tide. The surface remained dangerously slippery at the best of times. Johan Bruyneel's strategy was for the team to ride together as close as possible to the front of the peloton. He figured that a rider was sure to go down on the causeway. The Postal team would have a good chance of avoiding a massive pileup if they were in front. Armstrong took his director's advice.

And good advice it was. Not one, but two mass crashes on the causeway eliminated many riders, including Armstrong teammate Jonathan Vaughters. Several race front runners, one of them Michael Boogerd, did not crash but were delayed behind the fallen riders. Because of the narrowness of the causeway, they could not go around the accident scene. They were never able in subsequent stages to recover the lost time. Looking back, some analysts believed the race outcome was actually determined at this early stage.

Armstrong conserved his strength until Stage Eight, the year's second of three time trials. This course would be seven times longer than the prologue time trial. Riders would have to go flat out for over an hour. Armstrong had practiced it during team training camp, but in the early morning of race day he scouted the course one last time. This meticulous preparation

Jersey of Honor

The famed yellow jersey made its first appearance in the 1919 Tour de France. Race founder Henri Desgrange thought the bright, distinctive color would allow fans to more easily spot the leader as the peloton whizzed by.

The French words for yellow jersey are *maillot jaune*, pronounced my-oh zhoan. The yellow jersey is awarded every day of the race to the rider with the lowest cumulative time to that point. Immediately following the end of the stage, the overall time leader makes his appearance on the award podium. The yellow jersey is ceremoniously slipped on. He is handed a bouquet of flowers and a stuffed lion (a gift from a Tour sponsor). Two attractive young women kiss him on both cheeks. Then his name goes down in history.

paid off. So dominant was Armstrong's performance that he passed a rider who had taken off six minutes before he had. "You're blowing up the Tour de France," Bruyneel screamed into his radioear piece. Armstrong regained the yellow jersey. "I think I'm going to win this thing," he told his wife.[7] He now led overall by two minutes, twenty seconds.

The European press buzzed with disbelief at this turn of events. At a press conference on the rest day before week two, reporters incredulously asked how a cancer survivor could possibly be leading the Tour de France. "I was a halfway dead man," Armstrong acknowledged. But he had been cured by "the best doctors in the world, and I feel better now than I ever felt before."[8]

The press may have been agitated, but the peloton now seemed to breathe a collective sigh of relief. This new, improved Armstrong may have become good at time trials. However, he had never been a dominant mountain climber and would not be now. "I knew what the peloton was thinking," said Armstrong, "that I would fold."[9] They had no idea how long, hard, and intensely he had trained for this moment.

Stage Nine would be contested in the Alps. This rugged, scenic mountain range straddles France, Italy, and Switzerland. The course would scale three peaks before ending on a fourth mountain top in the Italian ski resort of Sestriere. Even in July, temperatures there can be frigid. Over the more than six hours of the ride, the competitors would brave blinding mist, freezing rain, and even hail.

Bruyneel's plan called for the Postal Service team to stay near the race leaders. The support riders would take turns pulling Armstrong up the mountains. He would particularly rely on two ferocious climbers, Americans Kevin Livingston and Tyler Hamilton.

These two would also be charged with "sitting on the wheel" of attackers. This tactic is the opposite of pulling. Instead of helping the attacking rider, they refuse to do any work, putting all the burden of cutting through the wind on the attacker. This also puts a heavy mental burden on the attacker. He knows that even if he can stay away from the pursuing peloton, the riders who are sitting on his wheel will be stronger in the finishing sprint and will likely beat him and steal his victory.

Armstrong later called his team's performance "superb."[10] They pulled him to the next to last climb, when Armstrong joined a small breakaway. Then Livingston and Hamilton clamped themselves to the wheel of the greatest remaining threat, to keep him from attacking. From that point on, Armstrong "showed no mercy," said Frankie Andreu.[11]

In the breakaway, Armstrong began to gain. He opened a gap between himself and most of the group. The gap grew. Only two riders remained ahead of him. Armstrong saw them glance back over their shoulders. As he pulled even, then ahead, he noticed their facial expressions. They seemed "incredulous," or stunned, he said.[12] He stayed a little ahead, waiting for them to counterattack but nothing happened. Armstrong knew they must be hurting. "And when they're hurting, that's when you take them," he said.[13]

Just before the finish line, Armstrong called back to Bruyneel in the team car, via his earphone radio. "How do you like them . . . apples!" he yelled.[14] When he crossed the line, he covered his face in disbelief. His lead over the field had grown by nearly four minutes—to six minutes, three seconds. Not only did he keep the yellow jersey in the mountains, he would never relinquish it again in 1999.

Stage Nineteen, the next to last, would be the third and final time trial. Only three riders in the history of the race had swept all three of a Tour's time

Armstrong is congratulated with a kiss on the cheek from his wife, Kristin (left), and his mother, Linda, after his Tour de France victory in 1999.

trials. Those three had also been five-time winners of the Tour de France—Bernard Hinault, Eddy Merckx, and Miguel Indurain. Armstrong made it his goal to sweep and join them. "I wanted to prove that the *maillot jaune* was the strongest man in the race," he said.[15] His mother flew to France for the event. Waving a small American flag, she followed immediately behind him on the course, riding in a race official's car. He won the time trial by nine seconds.

The next day, the Postal Service team swept onto the cobblestones of Paris's Champs-Elysees as the

"If you ever get a second chance in life for something, you've got to go all the way."

victors. "It was a dream come true for our team," said Frankie Andreu, "and for many Americans."[16] Armstrong was shocked at the number of American and Lone Star flags unfurled on the breeze. His mother had tried to warn him the previous day. "People in the U.S. are going crazy," she said. "I've never seen anything like this."[17]

More than fifty of Armstrong's Austin friends had hopped on planes to join him in celebration. They were "screaming, yelling, crying," said his longtime friend Bart Knaggs. The joy they felt for him was "just so intense, so rich."[18] Armstrong, struggling to hold back tears, said, "If you ever get a second chance in life for something, you've got to go all the way."[19]

That evening, a victory banquet was held in a magnificent Parisian art museum. On the Postal Service team tables lay curious but appropriate centerpieces—plates of apples. When Armstrong raised a flute of Champagne to toast his teammates, they returned his salute. Each man raised a fist, grasping a shiny, red apple.

8

NO FLUKE

"**He told me six months** before that race started," said journalist Sally Jenkins. "He said, 'Watch. I'm gonna win that race because nobody thinks I can.'"[1]

Lance Armstrong was predicting the outcome of the 2000 Tour de France. Many in the cycling community believed 1999 had been a fluke. Two of the sport's top champions had not competed in 1999. In 2000, German Jan Ullrich, the 1997 winner, and Italian Marco Pantani would return. So, once again, Armstrong set out to prove the whole world wrong.

Sally Jenkins, a sportswriter, cowrote Armstrong's autobiography *It's Not About the Bike*. Their book was published in May 2000. The inspirational story of Armstrong's comeback from illness to the peak of his sport, it shot to number one on the best-seller list. Armstrong had now become an A-list celebrity. He gave interviews on television's *Today* and *David Letterman* shows. He acquired a host of product endorsements. He even appeared on the Wheaties cereal box.

He also became a father. His son, Luke David, was born on October 12, 1999. Armstrong reveled in fatherhood. He even enjoyed hearing his boy cry, calling it "the wail of life." He was proud to be the parent of a fighter.[2] His wife observed that, having grown up fatherless, Armstrong could now play the role he wished someone had played for him. "In a way, he gets to go back and have a do-over," she said.[3]

"Watch. I'm gonna win that race because nobody thinks I can."

One other result of his 1999 Tour win was less uplifting. Some European journalists began to insinuate that only performance-enhancing drugs could have enabled Armstrong's victory. He had never even had a top-ten Tour finish before, they pointed out. Above all, he had barely escaped death from cancer a mere three years before.

Armstrong categorically denied any use of performance-enhancing drugs. He requested that the International Cycling Union release all his drug test results. He stated that he had won the race by working harder and smarter than his opponents. Nike, one of his sponsors, released a television commercial in which Armstrong spoke out. "Everyone wants to know what I'm on," he said. "What am I on? I'm on my bike six hours a day."[4]

Many Europeans wondered how Armstrong could appear so impassive on the bike. Other cylists' faces were masks of agony as they rode, their mouths gaping open. In fact, Europeans seemed to relish displays of suffering by their favorite racers. Tour lore celebrated riders who dragged themselves to the finish line despite intense pain. A French writer scoffed that Armstrong seemed like a "virtual human being . . . someone no fan can relate to or identify with."[5]

Armstrong, on the other hand, subscribed to the American concept of wearing a "game face." He chose to give nothing away to his opponents by displaying weakness or suffering. This intimidated riders who were suffering themselves. It also misled team directors with televisions in their follow cars. They were always on the lookout for tell-tale signs of cracking. Then they could communicate this to their riders by earphone radio. Dr. Craig Nichols, Armstrong's cancer specialist, expressed wonderment at the view of him as an automaton on wheels. "It's so funny to hear people talk that way," he said. "The fact is that no cyclist can have seen more pain than he has."[6]

Early in 2000, Armstrong, along with his wife and

infant son, moved once again to France. He promptly shed the trappings of celebrity. Every day, he kissed his family goodbye and went off to work. Of course, his workday consisted of six to seven hours of pedaling up and down mountains.

Then, "he comes home just like any other guy comes home," his wife told a reporter. "The first thing he always says is 'where's my boy!' He doesn't look tired. He looks so happy and peaceful." After a nap and high-carbohydrate meal, he had a few hours of relaxation. Then he went off to bed for the night—in an altitude tent, a low-oxygen environment that built up his lung power. In some ways, life during training resembled life "in a monastery," Kristin Armstrong said.[7]

By July, Armstrong was ready to go. And a good thing he was. "I started the 2000 Tour with a bull's-eye on my back," he said. His competitors were "all marking me."[8] He came in number two in the race's prologue time trial, losing by only one second. The Postal Service team then took second in the team time trial.

The first real test of the race came in Stage Ten, ending with an ascent of the monstrous Mount Hautacam in the Pyrenees Mountains. To Armstrong's delight, the day dawned to freezing rain. "Perfect," he said, looking out the window. "Suffering weather."[9] As the cold, windy, foggy day wore on, his rivals fell behind. At last, only he and Marco Pantani struggled up the slope side by side.

Armstrong had previewed the course in training several times. He knew just the spot to pick that would break Pantani by a show of strength. Sure enough, when he ground down on the pedals to lunge ahead, team director Johan Bruyneel's voice piped up in his earphone radio. "He's hurting," Bruyneel exclaimed. "He's coming off your wheel."[10] As planned, Armstrong's face gave no hint of the magnitude of his effort. "When I saw Armstrong," said a French rider, he appeared as if he were "descending a hill I was trying to scale."[11] This performance gained him the yellow jersey.

Jan Ullrich's team director all but conceded the race. "We know who the winner is already," he said.[12] Not so fast. During Stage Sixteen, Armstrong nearly made a fatal mistake. Over the previous few days, he and Marco Pantani had been verbally sparring in the

Colorful Jerseys

The yellow jersey is not the only one awarded at the Tour de France. A green jersey is worn by the rider with the most sprint points. Sprinting is the ability to accelerate with a sudden burst of speed, usually at the end of a flat stage. The "King of the Mountains" wears the polka-dot jersey by accumulating points awarded for being first over the top of each peak in the competition. This jersey was introduced in 1975 under the sponsorship of *Poulain Chococat*. The candy maker's products were wrapped in white paper with pink polka dots.

A white jersey is worn by the rider with the lowest cumulative time who is under twenty-five years of age. The reigning world champion may wear the rainbow jersey in competition. National time trial champions may also wear their national colors.

press. Pantani, nicknamed "the Pirate" because of his flamboyant appearance, accused Armstrong of showing disrespect to him. Armstrong responded by calling Pantani by his less-flattering nickname "Elefantino," a reference to his large, protruding ears.

Pantani later admitted that his strategy in Stage Sixteen was to destroy Armstrong, regardless of the consequences. He attacked early and amassed a substantial lead. Armstrong took the bait, despite Bruyneel's advice to let Pantani go. Armstrong pursued Pantani to the point of failing to pause at the stage's final feed zone. By doing so, he missed his last chance to eat energy snacks on the fly.

His body ran out of fuel. It became a supreme effort for him merely to pedal. He saw black spots before his eyes. "I bonked," he admitted. "That was the hardest day of my life on a bike."[13] Fortunately, he retained first place. The more-than-seven-minute lead he had built up compensated for a disastrous day. Armstrong apologized to his teammates that night. And the next morning, Pantani woke to cramps so severe that he withdrew from the race.

Three days later, Armstrong went on to win the final time trial with the second fastest time in Tour history. The Postal Service team entered Paris the victors. They were the only team to finish the race with all nine riders remaining. Photographs of Armstrong on the podium hoisting baby Luke above his head delighted fans worldwide. As the yellow-clad father grinned at his son, Luke, wearing a tiny yellow jersey himself, grinned back.

"Face it," Armstrong said to a journalist early in 2001, "if I ride as fast as I rode last year, I'll probably win every year." Armstrong, Bruyneel, and the Postal squad had now perfected the recipe for Tour de France success. A superbly fit lead rider, Armstrong, who was driven to win. A demanding team leader, also Armstrong, who asked no less of his teammates than he did of himself. A creative thinker and tactical genius, Bruyneel, as team director. A hand-picked team, focused and loyal, each with a role to play. Top-of-the-line equipment and support staff. "I'm not saying nobody will ever ride faster than me," Armstrong admitted. But it would only happen "because something has gone wrong with our formula."[14] The "blue train," as cycling fans referred to the Postal Service team, had begun to roll.

That was the hardest day of my life on a bike.

In April 2001, Kristin Armstrong was again pregnant—this time with twins. Luke had become a rambunctious toddler. He rode behind his daddy's bike in a rolling cart, wearing a helmet he loved so much that he refused to take it off. Armstrong coached Luke in anticipation of the Tour de France.

"Who's going to win?" he would ask.

Lance Armstrong rides with the U. S. and Texas flags down the Champs-Elysees avenue after winning his third straight Tour de France on July 29, 2001.

"DADDY!" Luke would shout.

Then, "What is Daddy's color?"

To which Luke would respond, "Yo-yo!"[15]

But initially, Armstrong's title defense at the 2001 Tour did not go as planned. Though he remained healthy, several teammates suffered crashes or other injuries. As the Tour entered the Alps, Armstrong was in 24th place. Team director Bruyneel suggested a daring and stealthy ploy for the first mountain stage. Armstrong would feign exhaustion and lure his rivals into counting him out. Then he would attack.

Shock rippled through the peloton as Armstrong's shoulders sagged and "pain" distorted his face. Television commentators and team directors in their follow cars asked each other what could be happening. Armstrong appeared to barely trudge on at the back of the pack. Then he and teammate Chechu Rubiera reached the foot of the legendary Alpe d'Huez climb.

"Vollebak [floor it]," Bruyneel told them.

"Watch the show," Armstrong responded.[16]

The sagging shoulders straightened. The poker face replaced the grimace. Armstrong and Rubiera tore ahead. As they passed arch-rival Jan Ullrich, Armstrong turned full around to stare long and hard into Ullrich's face. Behind the German's sunglasses he saw a picture of true pain. Satisfied, Armstrong stood up on his pedals and zoomed up the mountain. Fooling the peloton and giving Ullrich "the Look," as it went down in cycling history, was "my best day on the bike, hands down," said Armstrong years later. He called it "a true sporting high."[17]

In some sports, this deception might be considered unsporting and unfair. Not in cycling. Craftiness and guile are honored there as much as strength and endurance.

Despite this triumph, "yo-yo" still eluded Armstrong. He would gain it with a decisive win on the six-peak Pla d'Adet stage. On one of the downhill stretches Ullrich missed a sudden turn. He shot off the road at nearly fifty miles per hour, over what appeared to be a sheer cliff. Armstrong exercised the traditional right of the Tour champion. He ordered the peloton to ride slowly and wait until Ullrich's fate was known. Luckily, the German had landed safely on a grassy ledge. Miraculously uninjured, he lugged his bike up the bank and rejoined the race.

Armstrong then ordered the competition to resume, and he showed no mercy. By the end of the day, Armstrong had taken first place and he would never give it up. His win in 2001 was "my most aggressive . . . the one I wanted most" and "probably the most fun," he said.[18]

October 2, 2001, was the fifth anniversary of Armstrong's cancer diagnosis. Dr. Craig Nichols performed a series of tests on Armstrong to determine the status of his recovery. When he finished, Nichols

Lance Armstrong rides past supporters on the Champs-Elysees during the final stage of the Tour de France on July 28, 2002.

stated, "Your chances of ever having trouble with this again are in essence zero."[19] The Armstrongs celebrated with a gala party at their cabin in the hills above Austin. They called their hideaway property Milagro, Spanish for "miracle." Armstrong got himself a vanity license plate reading "OCT 2."

In November, Kristin Armstrong gave birth to identical twin girls. The couple named them Grace Elizabeth and Isabelle Rose. Despite looking alike, from infancy they acted differently. Grace's personality emerged as the more placid of the two. Isabelle, though, was "the image of me," said Lance Armstrong, "down to personality."[20]

The already hectic pace of the Armstrong household now revved up to frantic. Two-year-old Luke pleaded, "No more airplane. Stay home with me now" to his father.[21] Nevertheless, Armstrong traveled just as much, if not more. Commitments to sponsors and the now highly-successful Lance Armstrong Foundation demanded his time. Meetings and personal appearances kept him away from home for much of his youngsters' babyhoods.

Many people, including Armstrong, believed that the route of the 2002 Tour de France was designed to foil him.[22] Some fans had complained that when Armstrong built up an insurmountable lead, the race's final week became boring. Everyone knew too soon who the winner would be. To keep the suspense higher, tour officials scheduled some mountain stages closer to the finish line.

If their intention was "Lance-proofing," it did not work. The 2002 Postal squad was "the best team I have ever seen," said Johan Bruyneel.[23] To honor them, Armstrong wore his blue team jersey at the starting line. This defied Tour tradition, by which the defending champion wears his yellow jersey on the first day. From the outset Armstrong dominated as never before. In fact the 2002 was *less* suspenseful than previous years. Armstrong won the Tour de France by a shocking seven minutes, seventeen seconds. He felt a greater sense of achievement in this victory than the previous three, he said, because of "the sheer beauty of that team performance."[24] Late mountain stages had not slowed them down a bit. *Velo News*, a cycling magazine, calculated how long Armstrong had ridden without a teammate pulling him. It turned out to be an astounding mere fourteen miles. Such was the team's skill and dedication.

If their intention was "Lance proofing," it did not work.

Armstrong now became the fourth cyclist in history to win four consecutive Tour de France. The record for total overall victories, also held by four men, was five. Naturally, talk began of Armstrong tying, then breaking, the record. When a reporter asked him about it,

Armstrong reacted strongly. "Six?" he asked. "I don't talk about six. That's bad juju, man." But he stood ready and eager to tie. "You can't get to six without going through five," he added. "All I care about is five."[25]

9

BREAKING THE RECORD

To the shock of most people who knew them, Lance and Kristin Armstrong separated early in 2003. Lance Armstrong moved alone to his cabin at Milagro. At first, the couple underwent marriage counseling with the intention of salvaging their relationship.

Neither of the Armstrongs identified a single conflict or rupture in their marriage. Instead, both pointed to the cumulative effects of four years of travel, disruption, and stress from their whirlwind lifestyle.[1] Armstrong realized "the seize-the-day mentality that I carried with me from the illness doesn't always serve me well . . . Some things require patience."[2] Sadly, the counseling failed and the couple divorced by the end of the year.

Armstrong threw himself into training in Girona, Spain, his new European base. Without his family "I tried to tell myself that I was managing the situation . . . but it worked on me," he said. "Now things went wrong all at once."[3] He crashed in a race just before the Tour de France. Though not seriously injured, he arrived battered in Paris for the start of the 100th Anniversary Tour. He suffered hip tendinitis, and was doubled over from a stomach virus.

Armstrong placed seventh in the prologue time trial. Then he rode into a huge crash during Stage One. Luckily, he escaped with a few scrapes. After that, an historic heat wave struck Europe during the Tour with temperatures above one hundred degrees day after day. Across the continent, hundreds died. Though raised in the brutal sun of Texas, Armstrong suffered in the heat himself. "He was tired. He was having to push himself," said British cyclist David Millar. "It gave everyone hope."[4]

Then the Postal squad saw its first glimmer of good fortune in Stage Four's team time trial. Riding like "a flying blue wedge of speed," said Armstrong, the crew won.[5] He now moved up to second overall. His teammate, Victor Hugo Peña, had the best cumulative time at this point due to a terrific performance in the earlier individual time trial. Peña claimed the yellow jersey. During the final minutes of the stage,

Armstrong had urged Peña on by asking, "What color do you want to wear tonight? What color?"[6]

Peña "shouted in triumph" at the finish line, he remembered. "Then Lance embraced me."[7] He remained so excited by his achievement that he barely slept. The next day was Peña's twenty-ninth birthday. As he rode along in yellow he could see spectators pointing at him in recognition. One of the curious perks of the yellow jersey is that when the race leader needs to relieve himself, the peloton stops until he finishes. "At one point that day," Peña said, "I said to Lance, 'Can we stop [to pee]?' and he said, 'We do whatever the yellow jersey wants.'"[8]

Unfortunately, Peña's one-day reign as race leader did not prove a turning point for the Postal team. Armstrong himself gained the yellow jersey himself a few days later but he continued to struggle. During Stage Nine, the temperature soared to 104 degrees, causing the road surface to liquefy. When a rider's tires stuck to the tar and he fell, Armstrong swerved to avoid him. He flew off the road and into a freshly-plowed field. Looking up, he realized that the road made a U-turn. He could rejoin the race by crossing the field. So he bounced across the furrows and jumped across a ditch, bike in hand, to catch up. Happily, his tires stayed intact. "That may have been the luckiest day I ever had," said Armstrong.[9] A few days later, he lost an individual time trial to his longtime rival Jan Ullrich.

Dehydrated in the intense heat, Armstrong finished the day's race with a white ring of salt around his parched mouth.

By Stage Fifteen, he held the overall lead by a mere fifteen seconds over Ullrich. But Johan Bruyneel and Armstrong's Postal teammates never lost faith in him. Now was crunch time, Armstrong realized. "The Tour is over," he announced to them.[10]

Stage Fifteen was the climb in the Pyranees Mountains. Ullrich promptly attacked. Armstrong calmly stayed with him. Five hours into the course, Armstrong had lost sight of his rival. He heard Bruyneel's voice in his earphone radio say, "Ullrich is dropped."[11]

Full of confidence, Armstrong surged on. Just ahead of him he saw a fan twirling a yellow souvenir knapsack at the edge of the road. Before he could turn his bike, the knapsack tangled in Armstrong's handlebar, throwing him to the ground. Though bruised and dirty, he leapt to his feet and sped away. "Good," said coach and spectator Chris Carmichael. "Lance rides much better when he has some emotion."[12]

"At moments like these, he wants to devour the world."

Now at the rear of the peloton, Victor Hugo Peña caught a glimpse of the accident on a follow-car television. Then he watched his team leader "dance out of the saddle with incredible cadence," he said. "At last," he thought, "Armstrong is riding like Armstrong . . . At moments like these, he wants to devour the world."[13]

Armstrong expanded his lead to a still-slim one minute, seven seconds with that stage win. Ullrich then made a final stab at victory.[14] In the third and last individual time trial though, he crashed and skidded into a bale of hay.

Stepping down from the podium later that day,

Lance Armstrong with his wife, Kristin, their son, Luke, and twin daughters, Isabelle and Grace, signal five in honor of Armstrong's fifth straight Tour de France victory in Paris on July 27, 2003.

Armstrong was greeted by cycling legend Bernard Hinault. "Welcome to the club," said the five-time Tour de France winner, assuming Armstrong's upcoming victory. Though the Postal Team rode into Paris sipping champagne as the champions, Armstrong was dissatisfied with himself. "I'm coming back," he said, "but I'm not coming back to lose . . . This year's level was unacceptable."[15]

In October, Armstrong attended a charity fund-raising event in Las Vegas for tennis player Andre Agassi's charter school. He met the rock star Sheryl Crow at the party. She asked him if he would take her for a bike ride sometime. He kiddingly responded by requesting guitar lessons. The two began dating.

During the off-season, Armstrong gave more attention to his foundation than he could while competing. Now called the Lance Armstrong Foundation, it raised millions of dollars annually. It had become a major

The Greatest Ever?

Is Lance Armstrong the greatest cyclist of all time?

There is little doubt that he was the greatest Tour de France competitor, with the most overall victories and the most consecutive victories. However, Armstrong's great friend, the Belgian Eddy Merckx, is often considered the greatest cyclist of all time. He holds the records for most Tour de France stage wins, most days in the yellow jersey, and most stages in a single year.

Armstrong freely admits that he designed his post-cancer cycling career around Tour de France wins. He competed in relatively few other races. Merckx did no such thing. He was also a multiple winner of classic cycling events at other times of the year and in other countries, over the course of a long career.

funding source for cancer research. Foundation employees, at Armstrong's urging, had developed its direct service to cancer patients called the Livestrong program. It functioned as an online resource center. Its Web site gave answers to questions, connections to other victims and survivors, and information about new and experimental treatment options.

One of Armstrong's sponsors, Nike, had been making flexible plastic wristbands for its basketball stars to wear. Players would snap the wristband for good luck when they attempted a free throw. At a brainstorming session, a Nike employee had an idea. Why not make a yellow wristband emblazoned with the word "Livestrong"? The Foundation could sell it as a fund-raiser in the fight against cancer. Nike made an outright gift of one million dollars to the Foundation. Then they manufactured five million wristbands to be sold for one dollar each. Armstrong thought his sponsor was "incredibly generous" and "a little crazy" to make so many.[16]

Still, he began to wear one himself. Sheryl Crow wore one at her concerts. Soon, their pal Andre Agassi was seen wearing one at a tennis tournament. So were tennis pro Serena Williams and New York Yankee Derek Jeter. Several athletes sported them at the 2004 Summer Olympics. As a television camera zoomed in on a gold medalist, runner Hicham El-Guerrouj of

Morocco, *two* were visible on his wrist when he knelt to pray after his victory.

"It's amazing," said Armstrong, "beyond our wildest dreams."[17] Soon 100,000 a *day* were being bought. By 2005, an astonishing 50 million had been sold worldwide. That meant 50 million dollars for cancer treatment and research.

Wherever Armstrong appeared, cancer patients were drawn to him. At races, they often congregated around the Postal team bus, hoping for a glimpse, a word, a touch. Over the years, as his fame increased, it became more difficult for Armstrong to mingle with these special fans as he once had.

At a race in Portugal early in the 2004 European season, however, an attractive young woman and her husband approached several Postal team members for autographs. As they obliged, she told them how much she loved the sport, the team, and Armstrong. The next day she appeared again. This time Armstrong was present. When she saw him, teammate Michael Barry said, she seemed "ecstatic." As she spoke to Armstrong, she pulled off her wig to show her head bald from chemotherapy-induced hair loss. Armstrong hugged her, Barry remembered, and urged her to keep fighting.[18]

While the cancer community revered him, some in the cycling community vilified Armstrong. Since his first Tour de France victory in 1999, rumors and

Lance Armstrong and Sheryl Crow sit courtside during a basketball playoff game between the Houston Rockets and Los Angeles Lakers in Los Angeles in 2004.

unsupported accusations of drug use had never stopped. This despite his blood and urine being sampled by officials year-round, in surprise visits. Over the years, Armstrong had never tested positive for any illegal or performance-enhancing drug. The frustrated athlete himself requested that a clause be written into his endorsement contracts. If he ever tested positive for any banned substance, he would give all the money back. Still, the accusations continued.

Journalists took sides in the debate. One American

writer said, "After I watched Armstrong train . . . the only way I could be convinced that he uses illegal drugs would be to see him inject them."[19] In sharp contrast, two European journalists researched and wrote a book titled *L.A. Confidential.* Excepts were published in a French magazine a month before the 2004 Tour de France. The writers accused Armstrong of having used banned, performance-enhancing drugs in 1999. They quoted a former Postal team employee as saying Armstrong hinted to her that he did. She also claimed that she had retrieved unidentified pills for him and had disposed of syringes she claimed he had used. Even the book's coauthor, David Walsh, admitted that his evidence was "all circumstantial" and that "we don't actually prove anything."[20]

Armstrong responded that these charges were "absolutely, positively false." Asked by a reporter if he had ever used illegal performance enhancers he answered, "For the millionth time: I don't do that."[21] He instructed his attorneys to file suit against the book's authors and publishers in London and Paris.

Shortly before the 2004 Tour de France began, a journalist asked Armstrong if he was still angry enough to win. "It used to be said that anger was a big part of your drive," the journalist reminded him. "Oh, when I need to be [ticked] off," Armstrong replied, "I can still come up with something."[22]

No problem now. Armstrong was plenty angry

about the doping allegations. Now he viewed it as his "mission," he said, to strike back at his accusers by breaking the record and winning his sixth Tour. None of the previous five-time winners had done so after age thirty-one. The thirty-two-year-old Armstrong declared he was more interested in winning the race than becoming the record holder. Still, he admitted, "You do that, you make history. I'm no fool. That's a cool thing."[23]

And make history he did. Armstrong and his Postal Service team crushed the field with a victory margin of more than six minutes—six times 2003's slim margin. Armstrong won the prologue and six of the course's twenty stages. He made capturing an uphill time trial on the brutal Alpe d'Huez look easy.

At a team party on the eve of their entry into Paris, Armstrong joined his teammates in a chant of "Six! Six! Six!" Then they planted a bike helmet adorned with the horns of a Texas steer on the head of team director Johan Bruyneel. Amid the hilarity, Armstrong declared to a reporter, "This was as much fun as I've ever had in a bike race."[24]

The next day dawned bright and sunny. Armstrong and his team took a relaxing spin onto the Champs-Elysee. He repeatedly took both hands off the wheel to hold up six fingers for the cameras, flashing a wide grin. A half million fans packed the square. French, American, and Texan flags fluttered in the breeze, creating a rippling wave of red, white, and blue. Armstrong hoisted the winner's trophy above his head as the crowd roared.

A few minutes later, Armstrong took a phone call—from the president of the United States, George W. Bush. "You're awesome," the president said simply.[25]

10

LANCE'S LEGACY

Armstrong broke his own record the next year in the 2005 Tour de France. He won his seventh consecutive race. Tour officials gave him an historic opportunity to address the crowd, the first champion ever to do so. He spoke to his doubters. "I'm sorry you can't dream big, and I'm sorry you don't believe in miracles. This is the hardest sporting event, and hard work wins it. So vive le Tour!"[1]

This time Armstrong's children had attended the race to see his victory. Luke wore a yellow shirt. The twin girls, Grace and Isabelle, wore matching yellow sundresses selected by their doting grandmother Linda. She had accompanied them to Europe.

During the race Luke had become fascinated with the polka-dot jersey. This jersey is awarded to the "King of

Armstrong's Unique Contribution

How did Lance Armstrong and his team change professional cycling, especially the Tour de France?

Armstrong and his *directeur sportif* Johan Bruyneel painstakingly selected which team members rode in support at the Tour. Support riders must be ego-less, giving up their personal ambitions to the team and its leader. Bruyneel also balanced climbing specialists with flatland specialists in a new, calculated way.

Their most lasting contribution in retrospect seems amazingly obvious, yet they pioneered it. The Armstrong/Bruyneel teams were the first, and for years the only ones to train on the actual course where the Tour de France would take place.

Lastly, Armstrong brought an intensity, charisma, and will to win.

the Mountains," the best climber. Pink on a white background, it had caught the youngster's fancy. Luke eagerly followed the progress of Michael Rasmussen, holder of the polka-dot jersey. When Rasmussen repeatedly fell during the final time trial, Luke was worried. "Do you think Dad will stop and help him?" he asked his father's girlfriend, Sheryl Crow. "I don't think so," she answered. Luke also pointed out all spectators wearing the yellow Livestrong bracelet. "That's a friend of dad's," he'd say.[2]

When Armstrong walked to the victory stand to be acknowledged, his three children unexpectedly trotted along behind him. They acted as if it were the most natural thing in the world. "It was a special moment," Armstrong said. Luke, almost six years old, could now understand and would always remember the victory, Armstrong told an interviewer. In the past, his kids could not differentiate his work from play. After all, kids riding bikes are having fun. Now, they had seen him at work in a race. Now, they would "relate to what dad does for a living," and see him as "a winner," he said.[3]

"I really wanted to go out on top," said Armstrong later. "I know that the sport has given me way more than I ever thought it would. And it's time to move on."[4] After the race, Armstrong took his children on vacation to the beach in Europe. "His mission for the next six months," said Crow, "will be to spend as much time as possible drinking up his children's love."[5]

What would Armstrong do now with the rest of his life? He had much to offer. Armstrong is highly motivated, an accomplished leader, a multitasker par excellence. Possibilities in show business, commerce, and politics tempted him. He had a special ability to communicate a vision to the average person. Bono, of the rock group U2, reached out to Armstrong with advice. Bono was another celebrity who used the power of his name to do good. "Take a year," the singer and activist said. "Step back from your career. Really figure out what you want to do with your life."[6]

However, new doping charges abruptly interrupted Armstrong's period of reflection. Only a month after the Tour, the French sporting news journal *L'Equipe* blasted Armstrong. They reported the alleged results from re-testing of urine samples taken at the 1999 Tour. In the year of Armstrong's first victory there had been no method of testing for the illegal blood-booster EPO. Now that the test was available, the paper reported, it showed several athletes had tested positive for EPO that year. One of them was alleged to be Armstrong.

An outraged Armstrong, barely controlling his anger, appeared on CNN's *Larry King Live.* He called the French news story "preposterous." King asked him, "Can you unequivocally say you have never used an illegal substance ever?" To which Armstrong replied, "Listen, I've said it for seven years . . . longer than seven years. I have never doped."[7]

Armstrong then attacked the charges on several fronts. He pointed out that the allegations stemmed only from a news story based on anonymous reports. No sports governing body actually accused him of misconduct. Testing protocols established by the World Anti-Doping Agency had not been followed, he declared. The article stated that six of his samples from 1999 had tested positive. Since he had given seventeen samples during the 1999 Tour de France, why had the other eleven been negative?

Then he pointed to his performance in the years after 1999, when the test to detect EPO became available. In all subsequent years, he tested negative. "If you have such an advantage in '99 with this drug called EPO and they took it away from you in 2000, 2001, why are you still going fast?" he asked.[8]

The International Cycling Union launched its

Lance Armstrong runs in the New York City Marathon on November 5, 2006. Armstrong ran in the race to raise money for charity.

own investigation. Nine months later the union investigator, Dutch attorney Emile Vrijman, exonerated Armstrong "completely."[9] In fact, Vrijman said that the testing procedures used had been so improper and unscientific that they did not "constitute evidence of anything."[10]

During late 2005, Armstrong dabbled in several new ventures. He hosted a radio show on the Sirius satellite network. He gave motivational speeches. He hit the celebrity circuit of awards shows with musician girlfriend Sheryl Crow.

After having dated for two years, the couple announced their engagement in September 2005. Only four months later, though, they broke the engagement and parted. Then, a mere two weeks after the split, a routine mammogram showed that Crow had developed breast cancer. She underwent surgery to remove the tumors, followed by radiation therapy. Fortunately, the cancer was detected at an early stage. Doctors gave Crow a good chance for recovery. Said Armstrong, "Once again I'm reminded of just how pervasive this illness is, as it has now touched someone I love deeply."[11]

By no coincidence, Armstrong would spend the bulk of his first post-retirement year's work on the fight against cancer. "Making a significant difference in the battle" against the disease, he said. "That's how I make seven yellow jerseys look small."[12]

The yellow "livestrong" wristbands continue to symbolize the efforts of the Armstrong Foundation to wipe out cancer today.

First, he lobbied his former Austin neighbor, fellow cyclist, and admirer, President George W. Bush. Armstrong requested increased cancer research funding in the federal budget. Then his foundation sponsored a conference bringing together the brightest and most-innovative thinkers in cancer research. Armstrong and his staff posed questions to the gathered scientists. What if there were nothing hampering you? What would need to be done? Armstrong said little as the scientists brainstormed. He listened intently and took notes.

He also formed an endorsement partnership with American Century investments. Among this company's owners is the Stowers Family, who fund an innovative medical research facility of their own. "Ten years from now," said another American president, Armstrong's friend Bill Clinton, "we may say Lance's second career was greater than his first."[13]

Armstrong now lives full-time in Austin when he's not traveling for business. His house is within walking distance of his ex-wife's. Their children easily move back and forth between their parents, with bedrooms in both locations. Armstrong designed his son's new room, notable for its dinosaur murals. "My son has the coolest room of any [kid] in the world," he says.[14] No longer does Armstrong have to hear about his children's activities long-distance. Those days were "terrible," he told a reporter. "So now, being at home with them is just amazing."[15]

He has also had time to do simple things that a busy, world-class athlete and celebrity cannot do. After a Spring 2006 business trip to Los Angeles, he drove solo up the California coast on vacation. Rarely since his teen years had he traveled alone. "I was scared, but it was amazing," he admitted.[16] He has also dabbled in a variety of sports. He mountain bikes frequently and ran the 2006 New York Marathon.

"Not the next Lance. There's only one."

Armstrong has not forgotten the sport that made him famous. He continues his part-ownership of the Discovery Channel cycling team. He made a low-profile return to France for the second week of the scandal-ridden 2006 Tour.

A reporter once asked Bart Knaggs, Armstrong's friend since high school and now president of the Discovery Channel team, about the future of American cycling. Was the next Lance waiting to be discovered? he inquired. "No," Knaggs answered, "not the next Lance. There's only one."[17]

CHRONOLOGY

1971	Lance Armstrong is born in Dallas, Texas.
1989	Graduates from high school. Joins the U.S. National Cycling Team.
1992	Competes in Olympic Games at Barcelona. Turns professional.
1993	Wins American triple crown and World Championship. Becomes youngest winner ever of a Tour de France stage.
1995	Wins Classica San Sebastien and Tour Dupont.
1996	Diagnosed with testicular cancer. Treated with surgery and chemotherapy.
1997	Establishes the Lance Armstrong Foundation.
1998	Marries Kristin Richard. Returns to professional cycling.
1999	Wins Tour de France. Son Luke is born.
2000	Publishes *It's Not About the Bike*. Wins second-consecutive Tour de France.

Wins third-consecutive Tour de France. Daughters Grace and Isabelle are born. Five years cancer free.	**2001**
Wins fourth-consecutive Tour de France.	**2002**
Wins fifth-consecutive Tour de France. Divorces wife Kristin.	**2003**
Wins sixth-consecutive Tour de France.	**2004**
Wins final and seventh-consecutive Tour de France.	**2005**

CHAPTER NOTES

Chapter 1. Magnificent Seven

1. Austin Murphy, "Seven Samurai," *Sports Illustrated*, June 20, 2005, p. 50.
2. "Lance Armstrong Wants to Win a Seventh-Straight Tour de France So Badly That, This Year, He's Giving Up His Career to Do It," *Bicycling*, August 2005, p. 58.
3. Ibid.
4. Martin Dugard, *Chasing Lance* (New York: Little, Brown, 2005), p. 72.
5. Austin Murphy, "Uphill Racer," *Sports Illustrated*, July 25, 2005, p. 52.
6. Dugard, p. 113.
7. Ibid., p. 187.
8. Bob Ford, "Armstrong Repays a Dutiful Teammate," *Philadelphia Inquirer*, July 18, 2005, p. E4.
9. Dugard, p. 66.
10. Austin Murphy, "A Grand Finale," *Sports Illustrated*, August 1, 2005, p. 50.
11. Dugard, p. 235.
12. Ibid., p. 41.

Chapter 2. Iron Kid

1. Bill Strickland, "I Owe My Life to Cancer," *Bicycling*, November 1999, retrieved from EBSCOhost database (July 28, 2005).

2. Linda Armstrong Kelly, *No Mountain High Enough* (New York: Broadway Books, 2005), p. 80.

3. Ibid., p. 89.

4. Ibid., pp. 105–106.

5. Ibid., p. 104.

6. Lance Armstrong, *It's Not About the Bike* (New York: Berkley Books, 2000), p. 20.

7. Kelly, p. 107.

8. Armstrong, p. 23.

9. Ibid., p. 27.

10. Ibid., p. 23.

11. Geoff Drake, "America's Lone Star," *Bicycling*, May 1993, retrieved from EBSCOhost database (July 28, 2005).

12. Armstrong, p. 26.

13. Drake.

14. Kelly, p. 4.

15. Daniel Coyle, *Lance Armstrong's War* (New York: HarperCollins, 2005), p. 289.

16. Drake.

17. Kelly, pp. 161–162.

18. Ibid., p. 169.

19. Leigh Montville, "Breaking Away," *Sports Illustrated*, July 4, 1994, p. 54.

Chapter 3. Not the Next Greg LeMond

1. Austin Murphy, "A Grand Finale," *Sports Illustrated*, August 1, 2005, p. 46.

2. Bob Ford, "Armstrong Repays a Dutiful Teammate," *Philadelphia Inquirer*, July 18, 2005, p. E1.

3. Lance Armstrong, *It's Not About the Bike* (New York: Berkley Books, 2000), pp. 44–45.

4. Michael Spector, "The Long Ride," *New Yorker*, July 15, 2002, p. 50.

5. Bill Gifford, "The Man Behind the Man," *Bicycling*, May 2003, retrieved from EBSCOhost database (July 28, 2005).

6. Michael Barry, *Inside the Postal Bus* (Boulder, Colo.: Velo Press, 2005), p. 195.

7. Linda Armstrong Kelly, *No Mountain High Enough* (New York: Broadway Books, 2005), p. 179.

8. Armstrong, p. 50.

9. Geoff Drake, "America's Lone Star," *Bicycling*, May 1993, retrieved from EBSCOhost database (July 28, 2005).

10. Armstrong, p. 61.

11. Bill Strickland, "Lance," *Bicycling*, October 1999, retrieved from EBSCOhost database (July 28, 2005).

12. Armstrong, p. 61.

13. Drake.

14. Kelly, p. 181.

15. Armstrong, p. 63.

16. Layne Cameron, "Lance Armstrong: World Champion Cyclist," *Jack & Jill*, July/August 1994, retrieved from EBSCOhost database (July 29, 2005).

Chapter 4. The First Lance Armstrong

1. Leigh Montville, "Breaking Away," *Sports Illustrated*, July 4, 1994, p. 54.

2. Daniel Coyle, *Lance Armstrong's War* (New York: HarperCollins, 2005), pp. 177–178.

3. Geoff Drake, "Young Gun," *Bicycling*,

December 1993, retrieved from EBSCOhost database (July 28, 2005).

4. Ibid.

5. Geoff Drake, "America's Lone Star," *Bicycling*, May 1993, retrieved from EBSCOhost database (July 28, 2005).

6. *Current Biography, 2000* (New York: H.W. Wilson Co., 2000), p. 40.

7. Geoff Drake, "Lance's Lessons," *Bicycling*, July 1994, retrieved from EBSCOhost database (July 28, 2005).

8. Montville, p. 53.

9. Lance Armstrong, *It's Not About the Bike* (New York: Berkley Books, 2000), p. 66.

10. Drake, "Lance's Lessons."

11. Alan Shipnuck, "Tour de Armstrong," *Sports Illustrated*, May 20, 1996, p. 50.

12. Ibid, p. 48.

13. Linda Armstrong Kelly, *No Mountain High Enough* (New York: Broadway Books, 2005), p. 187.

Chapter 5. Cancer Picked the Wrong Guy

1. Linda Armstrong Kelly, *No Mountain High Enough* (New York: Broadway Books, 2005), p. 188.

2. Lance Armstrong, *It's Not About the Bike* (New York: Berkley Books, 2000), p. 11.

3. Ibid., p. 12.

4. Todd Balf, "Lance vs. Cancer," *Bicycling*, February 1997, retrieved from EBSCOhost database (July 29, 2005).

5. Austin Murphy, "A Grand Finale," *Sports Illustrated*, August 1, 2005, p. 47.

6. Nike television commercial, transcription by the author.
7. Murphy, p. 47.
8. Armstrong, p. 98.
9. Ibid.
10. Ibid., p. 99.
11. Ibid., p. 119.
12. Ibid., p. 146.
13. Ibid., pp. 148–149.
14. Balf.

Chapter 6. Viva Lance

1. Lance Armstrong, *It's Not About the Bike* (New York: Berkley Books, 2000), p. 5.
2. Michael Spector, "The Long Ride," *New Yorker*, July 15, 2002, p. 51.
3. Armstrong, p. 153.
4. Davis Phinney, "Racing for the Roses," *Bicycling*, July 1997, retrieved from EBSCOhost database (July 29, 2005).
5. Armstrong, p. 173.
6. Todd Balf, "He's Back and He's Pissed," *Bicycling*, January/February1998, retrieved from EBSCOhost database (July 29, 2005).
7. Scott Martin, "The Comeback Kid," *Bicycling*, May 1998, retrieved from EBSCOhost database (July 29, 2005).
8. Bill Strickland, "'I Owe My Life to Cancer,'" *Bicycling*, November 1999, retrieved from EBSCOhost database (July 28, 2005).
9. Armstrong, p. 198.
10. Ibid., p. 201.

11. Ibid., p. 202.
12. Strickland.
13. Leigh Montville, "Tour De Amerique," *Sports Illustrated*, August 9, 1999, p. 74.
14. "Forgive Us Father, For We Have Sinned," *Mountain Bike*, May 1999, retrieved from EBSCOhost database (July 28, 2005).
15. Armstrong, p. 202.

Chapter 7. The Yellow Jersey

1. *Lance Armstrong: Racing for His Life* (videorecording), A&E, 2000, transcription by the author.
2. Lance Armstrong, *It's Not About the Bike* (New York: Berkley Books, 2000), p. 226.
3. Ibid., p. 228.
4. John Wilcockson, *Lance Armstrong and the 1999 Tour de France* (Boulder, Colo.: Velo Press, 1999), p. 79.
5. Tim Laydon, "In Advance of Lance," *Sports Illustrated*, June 18, 2001, pp. A23–24.
6. Todd Strickland, "Lance," *Bicyling*, October 1999, retrieved from EBSCOhost database (July 28, 2005).
7. Armstrong, p. 237.
8. Wilcockson, p. 115.
9. Armstrong, p. 238.
10. Wilcockson, p. 122.
11. Ibid., p. 123.
12. Armstrong, p. 241.
13. Ibid., p. 242.
14. Ibid., p. 244.
15. Wilcockson, p. 163.

16. Ibid., p. 170.
17. Armstrong, p. 259.
18. *Lance Armstrong: Racing for His Life.*
19. Armstrong, p. 257.

Chapter 8. No Fluke

1. *Lance Armstrong: Racing for His Life* (videorecording), A&E, 2000, transcription by the author.
2. Lance Armstrong, *It's Not About the Bike* (New York: Berkley Books, 2000), p. 275.
3. *Lance Armstrong: Racing for His Life.*
4. Ibid.
5. Michael Spector, "The Long Ride," *New Yorker*, July 15, 2002, p. 58.
6. Ibid.
7. Ian Thomsen, "Heavenly Ascent," *Sports Illustrated*, July 24, 2000, p. 45.
8. Lance Armstrong, *Every Second Counts* (New York: Broadway Books, 2003), p. 40.
9. Ibid., p. 42.
10. Ibid., p. 43.
11. Thomsen, p. 42.
12. Ibid.
13. Michael Spector, "The Long Ride," *New Yorker*, July 15, 2002, p. 48.
14. James Startt, "Face It . . . I'll Probably Win Every Year," *Bicycling*, May 2001, retrieved from EBSCOhost database (July 28, 2005).
15. Armstrong, *Every Second Counts*, pp. 103-104.
16. Ibid., p. 110.

17. "The Playboy Interview: Lance Armstrong," *Playboy*, June 2005, retrieved from EBSCOhost database (Dec. 20, 2005).
18. Ibid.
19. Armstrong, *Every Second Counts*, p. 132.
20. Ibid., p. 141.
21. Ibid., p. 134.
22. Ibid., p. 174.
23. Kelli Anderson, "King of the Hill," *Sports Illustrated*, August 5, 2002, p. 36.
24. Armstrong, *Every Second Counts*, p. 194.
25. Rick Reilly, "Sportsman of the Year: Lance Armstrong," *Sports Illustrated*, December 16, 2002, p. 71.

Chapter 9. Breaking the Record

1. Eric Hagerman, "Force Majeure," *Outside*, June 2003, p. 120, and Lance Armstrong, *Every Second Counts* (New York: Broadway Books, 2003), p. 162.
2. Armstrong, p. 221.
3. Ibid., p. 232.
4. Kelli Anderson, "Tour de Lance," *Sports Illustrated*, August 4, 2003, p. 53.
5. Armstrong, p. 233.
6. Ibid.
7. Matt Rendell, *A Significant Other* (London: Weidenfeld & Nicolson, 2004), p. 86.
8. Ibid., p. 88.
9. Anderson, p. 53.
10. Armstrong, p. 239.
11. Ibid.
12. Anderson, p. 52.

13. Rendell, p. 133.

14. Anderson, p. 53.

15. Ibid.

16. Evan Smith, "Lance Armstrong," *Texas Monthly*, July 2005, retrieved from EBSCOhost database (July 28, 2005).

17. "Armstrong Sweats the Details," *Cyclingnews.com*, June 11, 2004, <http://www.cyclingnews.com/riders/2004/interviews/?id=lance_armstrong042> (January 4, 2007).

18. Michael Barry, *Inside the Postal Bus* (Boulder, Colo.: Velo Press, 2005), p. 42.

19. Michael Spector, "The Long Ride," *New Yorker*, July 15, 2002, p. 58.

20. S. L. Price, "Lance in France (Part 6)," *Sports Illustrated*, June 28, 2004, p. 50.

21. Ibid.

22. Hampton Sides, "Six-Shooter," *Outside*, July 2004, p. 94.

23. Price, p. 53.

24. Austin Murphy, "The Joy of Six," *Sports Illustrated*, August 2, 2004, p. 44.

25. "Armstrong's Joyride," *USA Today*, July 26, 2004, retrieved from EBSCOhost database (May 22, 2006).

Chapter 10. Lance's Legacy

1. "A Conversation with Lance Armstrong," *Charlie Rose Show*, PBS, August 2, 2005, retrieved from Lexis-Nexis database (October 10, 2005).

2. Ibid.

3. Ibid.

4. Ibid.

5. Austin Murphy, "A Grand Finale," *Sports Illustrated*, August 1, 2005, p. 46.

6. "A Conversation with Lance Armstrong."

7. "Interview with Lance Armstrong," *Larry King Live*, CNN, August 25, 2005, retrieved from Lexis-Nexis database (October 10, 2005).

8. Ibid.

9. Samuel Abt, "Lance Armstrong Is Cleared of Doping Charge," *New York Times*, May 31, 2006, retrieved from www.nytimes.com (May 31, 2006).

10. "Report Clears Armstrong of Doping," *Philadelphia Inquirer*, June 1, 2006, p. C2.

11. Michelle Tauber, et al., "Strong Enough," *People*, March 13, 2006, p. 56.

12. Austin Murphy, "The Next Stage," *Sports Illustrated*, May 8, 2006, p. 64.

13. Ibid.

14. Ibid., p. 69.

15. Tom Brokaw, "Lance Armstrong," *Men's Journal*, July 2006, p. 68.

16. Ibid.

17. Murphy, "A Grand Finale," p. 50.

FURTHER READING

Armstrong, Lance. *It's Not About the Bike.* New York: Berkley Books, 2000.

Armstrong, Lance. *Every Second Counts.* New York: Broadway Books, 2003.

Barry, Michael. *Inside the Postal Bus: My Ride with Lance Armstrong and the U.S. Post Cycling Team.* Boulder, Colo.: Velo Press, 2005.

Doeden, Matt. *Lance Armstrong.* San Diego: Twenty First Century Books, 2006.

Grabowski, John F. *People in the News: Lance Armstrong.* Minneapolis: Lucent, 2005.

Liggett, Phil, James Raia, and Sammarye Lewis. *Tour de France for Dummies.* Indianapolis: Wiley Publishing, 2005.

Rendell, Matt. *A Significant Other: Riding the Centenary Tour de France with Lace Armstrong.* London: Weidenfeld & Nicolson, 2004.

INTERNET ADDRESSES

The Lance Armstrong Fan Club official site
http://www.lancearmstrong.com

Unofficial Lance Armstrong Fan Club site, maintained by "Velogal," a.k.a. Sammarye Lewis, co-author of *The Tour de France for Dummies*
http://www.lancearmstrongfanclub.com

The Lance Armstrong Foundation official site
http://www.livestrong.org

The Discovery Channel Cycling Team official site
http://www.thepaceline.com

INDEX